Alan.

KEEP THE FAITH BABY

KEEP THE FAITH BABY

A close-up of London's drop-outs

KENNETH LEECH

LONDON SPCK 1973

First published in 1973
by S.P.C.K.
Holy Trinity Church
Marylebone Road
London NW1 4DU

Computerised origination by Autoset, Brentwood, Essex
Printed offset in Great Britain by
The Camelot Press Ltd, London and Southampton

The publishers regret that it has not been
possible to trace the copyright holder of
the photograph used on the jacket.

SBN   281   02717   X

Go in peace and love,
Serve God, serve the people,
Keep the faith baby,
You are the Liberated Zone.

from the Eucharistic Rite of
the Free Church of Berkeley

CONTENTS

PREFACE

Between 1967 and 1971 the drug scene in Britain exploded. These were years of very powerful and significant changes not only in the patterns of drug abuse but also in the whole field of youth culture. During these years, I was curate of the Parish of St Anne, Soho, the heart of the drug culture of London's West End, a parish containing Piccadilly Circus, Leicester Square, Carnaby Street, and the centres of the night life of the metropolis.

This book attempts to describe some of the more important events as they occurred, and to provide a personal commentary on them. It is intensely personal but does, I hope, portray events carefully and accurately.

I am grateful to all my friends who were around Soho during this period and whose influence is embodied in these pages.

KENNETH LEECH

1

SETTING THE SCENE

In 1967, when this story begins, I was not exactly a newcomer either to Soho or to the drug culture. My early acquaintance with problems of drug abuse had been in Stepney at the end of the 1950s when, as a student, I lived and worked in the notorious Cable Street district. Cable Street was a legend throughout the 1930s as the scene of anti-fascist battles, and throughout the 1940s and 1950s as a district of increasing violence. 'London's Harlem' was the Press's term while Dr Michael Banton called his study of it in 1955 *The Coloured Quarter*. Both descriptions were inaccurate, for coloured immigrants comprised a small percentage of the residents of the Cable Street area. But it became popular as a social centre, especially for West African seamen, and there are colourful descriptions of it in writings by Roi Ottley and Colin MacInnes. As the social centre of the London Docks, Cable Street contained the centres of traffic in marijuana in the late 1940s, and it was here in 1958 that I first encountered pot-smoking groups. My early contacts were with merchant seamen from Sierra Leone and Gambia, and later with Nigerians and Somalis. At no time during four or five years in Cable Street did I come across heroin addiction. I went to help in a Franciscan mission there in 1958 and from then until 1961 I taught English to Somalis and helped in a club for African seamen and in a hostel for new immigrants. These were the years of Father Joe Williamson's energetic campaigns against the appalling slum conditions in the western part of Stepney. Cable Street was a slum café quarter with a great deal of cultural activity and a tremendous amount of human misery. The experience of living there was of incalculable help to me in my subsequent ministry in Soho.

In 1964, after three years in Oxford—at Trinity College and St Stephen's House—I was ordained Deacon and began to serve in the parish of the Most Holy Trinity, Hoxton, at the northern tip of the East End. Hoxton, the heart of what formed, until the London Government Act, the Borough of Shoreditch, was an area of settled population with the lowest mobility rate of all the London boroughs. Here lived families whose descendants had been there since the middle years of the last century. It was while I was working in Hoxton that my involvement with drug abusers grew and intensified, from three separate directions. The first was through two young heroin addicts in the parish who were in touch with a group of older addicts in North London, some of whom were Canadian refugees. These young heroin addicts were fairly untypical of Hoxton youth, most of whom were not acquainted with the opiates or any intravenous drugs. The second direction from which my contact with drug abusers came was the group of youngsters connected with a local experimental café project. Most of these, by 1964-5, were drug users, smoking cannabis and experimenting with amphetamines. Their sources of supply were Old Montague Street in Whitechapel, (one of my old haunts from Cable Street days) for cannabis, and the West End clubs for pills. Then, thirdly, I found that I was regaining contact with old friends in the Cable Street scene, some of whom had become heroin addicts during the years in which I had been away. Derek Cox, an exceptional youth worker, had come to work in Spitalfields soon after I had left, and he was closely in touch with the cafés in Old Montague Street and Brick Lane to which many of the old Cable Street clientèle had moved.* Hoxton was midway between the drug traffic area of the East End and that of Islington, and during 1965 and 1966 I found an increasing number of young addicts coming my way.

There were two people at this time who were most aware of, and in close touch with, the new addict society in the East End: Derek Cox, and Geoffrey Buckland, then a curate at Christ Church, Spitalfields. Christ Church was a Hawksmoor edifice whose rebuilding caused heated controversy in 1964. But its clergy were more concerned with human beings than with buildings, and the Crypt was opened as a rehabilitation programme for crude spirit alcoholics. These alcoholics gathered round Commercial Street and Fournier Street and in 'Itchy Park' (Christ Church Gardens) which, since the nineteenth century, had been a centre for the homeless derelicts. The drug takers were mainly found a little further to the East, in Brick Lane and the streets which ran off it. Old Montague Street in particular was a major distribution centre for cannabis and amphetamines. Very few East End doctors, however, were involved in the prescribing of heroin, and the emerging group of junkies in the Whitechapel and Spitalfields districts were getting their prescriptions from a doctor in West London. It was not difficult to trace the early spread of heroin addiction in the East End, through person-to-person infection, to the prescribing of this doctor. In 1966 the East End Drug Dependency Group was set up under the chairmanship of Dr C.R.B. Joyce, Reader in Psychopharmacology at the London Hospital Medical College. Dick Joyce played a very important co-ordinating role in bringing together workers in

* For a good account of Derek Cox's work, see his *A Community Approach to Youth Work in East London* (1970).

different disciplines in the East End who were concerned with problems of drug abuse. As a pharmacologist and psychologist, he was in a unique position at the London Hospital to act as a bridge between the medical and psychiatric world, and that of youth workers, social workers and others who were involved with the street addict.

In November 1965 the Second Report of the Inter-departmental Committee on Drug Addiction—the Brain Report—was published. Its main conclusion was that a small group of physicians in London was responsible for the epidemic of heroin addiction (paragraph 11). The Report continued: 'The evidence further shows that not more than six doctors have prescribed these very large amounts of dangerous drugs for individual patients, and these doctors have acted within the law and according to their professional judgment' (paragraph 12). It recom-mended (paragraph 22) the setting up of specialized treatment centres in the London area 'as soon as possible', and the limitation of prescribing of heroin for addicts to doctors on the staff of such centres (paragraph 26).

I felt then that the report was both naive and superficial in its analysis of drug addiction, and hopelessly narrow in its terms of reference. Paragraph 40 was the work of a genius: 'Witnesses have told us that there are numerous clubs, many in the West End of London, enjoying a vogue among young people, who can find in them such diversions as modern music and all-night dancing. In such places it is known that some young people have indulged in stimulant drugs of the amphetamine type.' In these words the whole complexity of the pill scene in Soho was digested into two sentences whose sentiments can only be described as archaic in the extreme.

As a result of the publication of the Brain Report I wrote a letter to *The Times* in which I expressed some of the fears of those of us who were working within the drug scene.

> The actual phenomena of drug traffic receives hardly any treatment in the Report: the word 'pusher' does not appear throughout its pages. A whole dimension has thus been omitted. The 'escalation' thesis, that the use of cannabis may lead to addiction to hard drugs, is mentioned, and you, Sir, in your leader of November 25th point out that 'progression from amphetamines and marihuana to heroin addiction can . . . be quicker than the ill-informed may realize'. But in neither case is it pointed out that one reason why this may happen is that in many places the pushers of both types of drug are the same people.

I do not now believe this statement to be true, though there was some evidence for its truth in 1965. In the early days of growth of drug cultures, cannabis, amphetamines, and heroin might be found in close association in the illicit traffic. But as the distinct drug-using groups emerge, this association ceases to apply. Today the sources of supply for cannabis and heroin are quite different, and the pushers are not the same. The argument for escalation by social contact does not therefore stand up to analysis.

However, it was an argument which, in common with other observers, I put forward at this time. On 7 March 1966 I gave a lecture on adolescent drug abuse in a London University extra-mural course. During this I referred to the dangers of involvement of cannabis and heroin users in a common subculture. Most teenagers who smoked pot did not progress to heroin, but, I argued, where progression did occur, it was due to social factors. I suggested therefore that there was a strong, if not an overwhelming, case for legalizing cannabis, in order to cut the link which leads to heroin and to incalculable human misery.

The following day the lecture was reported in *The Times* under the headline, 'Make marijuana legal, says curate'. On 9 March, Dee Wells delivered a violent and excited attack on me in the *Sun*, in which she accused me of being starry-eyed and ignorant of reality. Her article was a fairly good example of the kind of irrationality and hysteria which discussions about cannabis aroused, and still arouses, and it included a number of the popular misconceptions about the drug scene. 'Marijuana may be innocent. But it leads to heroin', she protested with indignation. I still find people quoting garbled versions of that lecture at me. An accurate version of the relevant sections of it was printed in Alan Bestic's *Turn Me On Man* (1966) and it looks very mild today, but at the time it brought considerable abuse, anonymous letters, and angry attacks from many sides.

In November 1966 I wrote a further letter to *The Times* which was again given prominent position, on 9 November under the headline, 'A year after the Drugs Report'. From both official and non-official sources, I later learnt that the impact of this letter was far greater than I had anticipated or realized then. In the letter I drew attention to the lack of official action as a result of the Brain Report.

The Minister of Health's notorious statement of August 2nd about treatment centres was received by doctors, social workers and addicts with cynical laughter or with despair. Those who daily face the problems of the young drug-taker are finding the obstacles almost insurmountable: hours and days spent ringing round hospitals for admissions; refusals, evasions, and interminable delays; addicts whose condition deteriorates and parents whose hearts are broken; doctors who refuse to prescribe, and doctors who prescribe with almost criminal irresponsibility; and an overwhelming sense of hopelessness and despair among those who know the drug scene closest.

I went on to point out three areas in which changes had occurred in the year since the Report.

First, the widespread reluctance and refusal of GPs throughout London to prescribe heroin and cocaine, even under carefully controlled conditions, coupled with the opting-out of several well-known doctors, has led to a worsening state of affairs.

The small group of 'junkies doctors', whose names and addresses are known to everyone working in the field, have inherited a situation which is now beyond control. While some medical sources have dried up, others have exploited the situation.

Secondly, it was inevitable that, given the post-Brain situation, the black market would develop. The latest report from the Home Office to the United Nations comments (paragraph 37) on the 'significant increase . . . in the numbers of addicts who have obtained their drugs entirely from unknown sources.' The same report insists that 'the illicit traffic in narcotics . . . is not extensive in the United Kingdom,' but how long will this remain the case?

The patients in the Salter Unit at Cane Hill Hospital, in their critique of Brain, warned that 'there is already in the wings, waiting its opportunity, the efficient and well-tried Mafia organization, eager to exploit a situation in which heroin is difficult to obtain.' There is no doubt that criminals have already moved into the black market in drugs, and many experts warn of the likelihood of professional syndicates on American lines trying to take over the controls.

Thirdly, while the relative absence of any 'drug subculture' is a characteristic of the English scene most frequently seized upon, this is becoming less true every day. The underworld is spreading to embrace kids on the 'pot and pills' fringe, spreading into new areas geographically, spreading socially and economically through sections of working-class urban delinquency.

The situation can be exaggerated and distorted, but it is serious enough. What is to be feared is that official reaction will be repressive and negative. So far, the results of the Brain Report have been almost entirely negative and bad. Since Brain, the situation has got worse, not better. And perhaps most frightening of all is the fact that many of our best workers in the areas of infection are coming to feel that they are banging their heads against a brick wall. Paralysis, like addiction itself, grows like a cancer and destroys.

This letter coincided with the disappearance from the heroin scene of a well-known GP in West London, and on 15 November, *The Times* published a letter from Dr A.J. Hawes, in which he drew some ominous conclusions from recent happenings:

One of the prominent 'junkies' doctors' has just thrown up his addicts' practice in the past few days. I cannot blame him, but the result has been to throw about eighty heroin and cocaine addicts on the open market which usually means the black market. In the past forty-eight hours I have had ten new applicants for supplies, whom I have had to turn away from my door—most regretfully. . . . The most threatening portent is that addicts are telling me that there is plenty of the stuff to be had on the black market even though the source from over-prescribing doctors is drying up.

It looks as if big business which has been waiting in the wings for so long has now taken over the stage and is playing the lead. So we may look for an explosion in the teenage addict population as the months go by.

A few weeks later, on 8 December 1966, I published a lengthy article, 'Danger on the Drug Scene' in the *Daily Telegraph,* in which I expanded some of the points made in the letter.

The Brain Committee was extremely narrow in its terms of reference, and its members had very slight knowledge of the drug scene. Only in paragraph 40 did it touch on the social aspects, and this was in language so archaic and naive that it reduces not only addicts and doctors but intelligent teenagers wherever it is read to hysterical laughter. What has happened in the year since Brain? At the official level, almost nothing. On August 2nd the Minister of Health, replying to a Commons question, said that 'there are already centres for the treatment of addicts, and more beds would be made available if the demand increases.' In a private letter to me dated August 19th the Ministry claimed that 'there are thirty or so hospitals in the London area which accept drug addicts for treatment.' These statements are ludicrous misrepresentations of the truth as anyone knows who has ever tried to get one addict into hospital: evasions, equivocations, and interminable delays are the order of the day, while the addict's condition deteriorates and his family are heart-broken.

Although I did not realize it then, these words were to be the beginning of a long campaign to obtain more satisfactory treatment facilities.

2

SUMMER OF LOVE

Summer 1967 was like bright sunshine before a terrible storm. It was known as the 'Summer of Love'. Love, peace and brotherhood were in the air. In London, Scott Mackenzie's record *San Francisco* was at the top of the hit parade, and spoke of 'gentle people with flowers in their hair'. There was a vision of a paradisal state where beautiful, non violent flower children grooved, dropped LSD and made love in an atmosphere of gentleness and peace. The Beatles' song, *All you need is love* summed up the prevailing mood. But for me the vision was soon to be buried under the needles and the crushed Methedrine ampoules as that freaky summer gave way to a hard and destructive winter.

It was during that summer of love that I moved into the Parish of St Anne, Soho, in the West End of London. Although I did not become its Assistant Curate until November, I took up residence in July and during the summer months I found myself living in Kingly Street, a small street parallel to Carnaby Street. Carnaby Street represents the commercial exploitation of the psychedelic movement. In that summer it rang with beads and bells, and terms like 'hippy' and 'turn on' became widely used. *International Times* was sold in the streets. A Beatles LP proclaimed, in words from the Tibetan Book of the Dead, 'Turn off your minds, relax and float downstream. This is not dying'. There was a sense of hope, a mood of peaceful tolerance, as the Soho streets were thronged with the flower children and their message of love. Like some new prophetic figures they preached their gospel of peace and smoked pot with tranquillity.

By the time that I moved into Soho I was fairly well acquainted with the West End drug scene and with the clubs which were used by drug-takers. There were two main groups of clubs: the big discotheques, some of which had live groups performing, which advertised in the musical press and gathered large numbers of teenagers; and the small, all-night 'coffee clubs' which catered for a more restricted, perhaps subcultural, group, with heavier drug involvement. The East End youngsters whom I knew tended to go for the big clubs, though some of them, including homosexuals, were attracted to the smaller ones. The drug traffic in these clubs was principally in amphetamine tablets, Dexedrine (dexamphetamine sulphate) and Drinamyl (dexamphetamine sulphate and amylobarbitone) being the most popular. Drinamyl had been produced in 1951 by Smith, Kline and French, and was an amphetamine-barbiturate mixture. It became known as 'purple heart' although it was, in fact, blue and triangular. Abuse of Drinamyl reached epidemic proportions in Soho in 1963, and the publicity led to the Drugs (Prevention of Misuse) Act 1964. But the Act was not particularly effective because it included no controls on manufacture, distribution or records of sales, and the traffic continued unabated. We found that high-dose amphetamine abuse was commonly associated with a very disturbed, sexually confused group of young people who tended to concentrate in certain clubs in the northern part of Soho, and, with the cooperation of the managements, a group of us began to sit around in some of these clubs and to establish points of contact within them.

About the same time that I started my own club work, Barbara Ward of the Soho Project began to operate as a detached youth worker in the small clubs, as well as in some coffee bars and amusement arcades. She was an experienced youth worker who had worked in the Teen Canteen in the Elephant area of South London, and in Hoxton, and she was able to establish herself fairly quickly within the groups of drifting young people. The idea of the Soho Project was to provide a mobile youth worker who could act as a liaison between the young people around Soho and the facilities of the youth service. In 1969 Carol Bohnsack, an American, joined Barbara, and in 1970 the Project took over offices in Charing Cross Road and changed both the methods and scope of its work. But in the summer of 1967 the club contacts were at an early stage of experimentation.

1966 and 1967 were years in which various individuals began to concern themselves with making contacts with the socially isolated and 'outsiders'. In the East End, Sally Trench, who subsequently wrote up her personal version of events in *Bury Me In My Boots,* started to move around the Stepney bomb-sites. In the West End, Vic Ramsey was drawing large crowds at his evangelistic meetings in the basement of Orange Street Chapel, not far from Soho, and was making links with the Trafalgar Square beatniks. In Soho, these were the years of Judith Piepe, a small German, middle-aged woman, who for several years operated as a freelance 'social worker' in some of the clubs. Judith was a colourful, extrovert figure, and became known to a wide audience by introducing the songs of Paul Simon to the British public in a series of talks on 'Five to Ten' in Holy Week, 1965. Towards the end of 1966 Judith appeared in a TV documentary 'Outcasts and Outsiders' in which scenes were taken in Soho clubs and some of the problems associated with homosexuality and drug abuse were discussed. The programme attracted a great deal of attention and probably brought a number of people around the country to some awareness of the needs of the isolated and outcast. My own feeling, however, was that the programme was a mistake, both because it focussed excessive attention on the work of one individual in a field where publicity can threaten very delicate and confidential relationships, and also because it offered a rather romanticized and sentimental view of the Soho area. It is always tempting to obscure the hard and complex problems of alienated youth beneath the language of pietistic and moralizing songs or slogans about involvement and care. However, Judith did very valuable work in Soho, and was helpful in introducing a number of us to the clubs where she had been working. By the summer of 1967 she had virtually withdrawn from this work, though she maintained a close contact with the folk clubs.

My own initial contacts were with a club frequented by young male homosexuals off Wardour Street. The club opened at 9.00 p.m. and stayed open until about 3.00 a.m. and all night on Fridays and Saturdays. About half a dozen of us felt that some kind of built-in welfare service was needed, and, as the management was keen to encourage this experiment, we set up a management and welfare committee of which I became Chairman. For a while during the summer we ran an advice service during the daytime, but the bulk of counselling and help was given, casually and informally, during the night. The idea was very simple: it was merely to provide a few people who would be available, sitting around the club, willing to talk and discuss problems in a non-authoritarian accepting manner.

The clientele of the club were mainly young, and were either homosexual or experimenting with homosexuality. The average age was about 18—19. There were at this time only a few heterosexual girls, and a large number of 'chickens', that is, very young, pretty boys who were acquired and used by the older ones. Promiscuity was normal, and relationships changed very rapidly. The kids were always 'falling in love', acquiring new 'affairs' (which lasted for a whole week!), and having endless dramas. Clothes and money were often crucial in the creation of new affairs. This period was really the screaming peak of the young homosexual clothing industry, and frequently I got the impression that it was more a matter of falling in love with a boy's clothes than with him as a person. The atmosphere in the club, as in many young gay clubs and bars, was superficially light-hearted, girlish and hysterical. Most conversations were about sexual exploits, and were a combination of fact and fantasy, where the borderlines between the two became very blurred.

One girl who was well known on the London gay scene in 1967 made some very perceptive comments about it. 'The people on the scene now are all very young or they're all old, there's no in-between . . . they're all either very very young and been going for about six months or a year and think they know it all, think they're beautiful, but after a year they suddenly go to pieces . . . after having various affairs, VD, etc . . . find they're spotty and aged and can't cope . . . I don't think anybody grows up on the gay scene at all . . . Whether they're a boy or a girl. They never grow up.' It was very much the adolescent acting-out of a homosexual role which dominated the life of this club, and it was against this background that any help would be offered.

Use of amphetamines by kids in the club was closely related to the confusion about sexual identity. There was as much boasting about the number of pills consumed as about the number of sexual acts. In fact, it was arguable the amphetamine highs were more pleasurable than sex to many of the youngsters, or at least that it was only when they were 'blocked' that they could act out their homosexual role. The maintenance of a 'camp' image was essential to the life-style of the club, and amphetamine use helped to create the artificial security in which this was possible. 'Contact highs' became very real in this highly charged atmosphere: whether or not the pills made you high, you *had* to feel and act high! So one got a crazy, artificial world in which conversation revolved round pills, affairs and clothes (on the high side) and frustration, paranoia and suicidal feelings (on the come-down.) Paranoid delusions and fears of persecution were common, and were increased by the spread of Methedrine. I remember keeping one young pillhead overnight in the flat. He spent most of the night searching in the cupboards for policemen, screaming at the non-existent crowds from the window, and ended the night at 5.00 a.m. by telephoning the West End Central Police Station to complain that I was attempting to 'lace' his coffee with LSD! During amphetamine 'horrors' the kids would see small insects or 'meth bugs' crawling all over them, and would exhibit terrific fears of being pursued by the police. We found, however, that those who used this and other clubs tended to leave the West End and the pill scene when they began to come to terms with themselves sexually and emotionally, and by 1970 it was noticeable that most of them had left.

The incidence of sexually transmitted disease was high among these pill users, though not among the 'junkies'. Drug addiction and sexually transmitted diseases do not go well together, partly because intravenous drug use is often a substitute form of sexual activity. A study of the patients under the age of thirty in the VD clinic which served Soho showed that only 18 per cent had drug experience. We did find, however, among the young homosexuals that promiscuous sexual activity and the use of amphetamines were very commonly associated. Many of the young 'chickens' were afraid of attending the clinic, but equally worried that they might have gonorrhoea, and the demand for antibiotics added a new dimension to the circulation of brightly coloured capsules! Several colleagues of mine, two of them psychologists and one a male nurse, operated a very helpful informal advice centre on VD and were able to link many of the boys with the local clinic.

A great deal has been written about the increase in sexually transmitted disease. International travel has added a number of difficulties to the management of the problem since it is often hard to trace the contacts, especially in the case of syphilis where it is the more necessary. In Soho there seem to be three principal factors involved: high promiscuity among many young people of both sexes; the concentration of promiscuous male homosexuals within the central area; and the widespread use of the West End 'call girl' rackets. I doubt whether prostitutes play much role in the spread of infection today. The men who use the West End prostitutes include those in search of abnormalities and deviations; those who are too shy to make deep relationships with women but might use prostitutes' services several times a year; and those who are in a hurry and go for a 'one nighter'. The call girl system, which is well organized and operates by telephone, caters particularly for overseas visitors, and there is a good deal of VD among this group. The young people with whom I was involved were promiscuous and did not take great care, and some would indulge in casual, amateurish prostitute activity around the clubs, coffee bars and amusement arcades.

One of the results of Judith Piepe's TV programme was that a young doctor, Ian Dunbar, offered his services to us to do voluntary medical work in Soho. At first Ian began to visit one of the clubs and was able to advise a number of young people on medical problems. But after a while we felt that it would be more valuable if he were able to take on a small number of heroin addicts as NHS patients. So in December 1966 a small clinic was opened on three evenings each week at St Anne's House. This ran for just over a year until the Dangerous Drugs Act 1967 came into effect and the patients were transferred to the new treatment centres. Ian Dunbar was a sensitive and dedicated physician, one of the few doctors who, within the National Health Service, were prepared to give time and care to heroin addicts. He started to use simple group therapy methods with his addict patients, whose number grew to about two dozen.

One of the controversial aspects of Ian Dunbar's work at St Anne's was his use of one of the medical preparations of cannabis, cannabis tincture, in the treatment of addiction. He originally used cannabis tincture as a 'weaning' drug. However there were accusations from some sources that such prescribing amounted to an indirect 'legalization of cannabis' since it was well known that some patients would 'cook up' the medicine, that is, pour the liquid over tobacco leaves, allow the alcohol content to evaporate, and smoke the residue. Dunbar explained the use of the drug in a talk at St Anne's on 31 August 1968:

> Over the last nine months I have prescribed tincture of cannabis quite freely to several hundred people. They can be divided into two groups. The first group are patients under treatment, with cannabis used like any other drug as a therapeutic aid. I feel that the effects of cannabis are in many ways similar to LSD but very much gentler. I use it as a psychotherapeutic facilitator. It seems to help patients get insight into their problems. The second group are people who have been smoking

cannabis abroad or who had to obtain it on the black market. I prescribed cannabis to them so that I could meet them in my consulting room, talk to them, find out what sort of people they are and learn of their aims, ambitions and outlook on life. This group was by far the larger and numbered about two hundred.

He noted also the existence of a smaller group with 'a deep sense of futility and rebellion' who were 'high risk cases for heroin addiction'. 'By prescribing cannabis for them, which they are going to buy on the black market anyway, they are at least being kept under observation. This is one of the first steps in preventive medicine.'

What Ian Dunbar was doing in fact was to apply the same principle to cannabis which the British medical profession applied to heroin: that it was preferable to prescribe the drug and thus keep it under medical observation than to allow black market forces to operate freely. However, his use of cannabis aroused a great deal of hostile criticism, and on 10 January 1969 the Recorder of Oxford, in a test case, ruled that if cannabis tincture is poured on tobacco and allowed to dry, what remains is cannabis resin and is therefore illegal. The judgement has interesting implications for cough mixtures which leave a sticky residue round the rim of the bottle!

After the clinic in Soho closed, Ian Dunbar became increasingly interested in the medical care of young hippies and, with two colleagues, in January 1969, he set up a kind of hippy family doctor service in premises in Notting Hill. It was a pity that this did not develop for financial and accomodation reasons, for he was one of the few doctors who was in touch with a significant section of pot-smoking, drop-out youth, for whom the provision of medical care within a framework sympathetic to their culture was, and is, fragmentary.

At this time too, various organizations were being formed in response to the 'growing problem of drugs'. One of the earliest of these was a body called the National Association on Drug Addiction. It was very short lived and contributed nothing of value, and there must be few workers in the field who regret its death, but it provided the basis for a national organization to co-ordinate efforts and information. It was followed by the Association for the Prevention of Addiction (APA), originally known as the Association of Parents of Addicts, formed in 1967. This organization had a temporary headquarters in St Anne's House from 1968 to 1969 when it moved to the nearby Covent Garden area. APA developed out of an article in the *Guardian* of 24 February 1967, entitled 'My son takes heroin', in which a mother appealed for an association of parents who would be able to help each other. By 1971 the APA had branches throughout the country and was involved both in educational work and also in the setting up of short-stay hostels and rehabilitation facilities.

Another body which came into existence in 1967, and with which we have had very close contact from the start, is Release. Release was originally set up to help young people who were arrested for drugs offences, but it later found itself involved in a wider area of social provision within the emerging Underground. Its original organizers, Rufus Harris and Caroline Coon, are both close friends of mine, and we have been able to co-operate both in individual cases and also in several large scale projects, such as the club 'Implosion', sponsored by Release, on whose committee I served, and the provision of welfare facilities at the Isle of Wight pop festival in 1970. In the early days of 1967-8 we found that Release and St Anne's overlapped considerably in their care of individual people. But as the drug scene spread geographically, the Notting

Hill area developed its own distinctive cultures, which were quite different from those of Soho. Gradually we found ourselves moving apart insofar as we were being heavily overloaded with the problems of individuals, but we continued to maintain regular exchange of ideas and information.

Since 1967-8 the growth of voluntary organizations in the drug field and related fields has been very striking. Some older bodies too have become involved with problems of drug abusers. Broadly speaking there are four main groups of organizations who work in this field. First, evangelical Christian groups including old-established societies like the Salvation Army, Church Army, Silver Lady, London Embankment Mission, and so on; and the more recent groups, mainly inspired by David Wilkerson's work in the United States. Secondly, communities and groups which stand within the Christian tradition such as the Simon Community, St Mungo's Community, Samaritans, and some religious orders, the best known of which is Spelthorne St Mary. Thirdly, various social work-orientated bodies such as St Martin-in-the-Fields Social Service Unit, APA, New Horizon, the National Association of Voluntary Hostels, and so on. Finally, there are the groups which have emerged out of the Underground itself such as Release, BIT, Gandalf's Garden, Street Aid, Solarium and various communes, centres and fringe mystical groups.

A major problem which confronts all voluntary groups working in the drug field is that of co-ordination. The cries for co-ordination in social work go back many years. In 1910 the Consultative Committee for the Homeless Poor attempted to co-ordinate activity in the field of vagrancy and there have been numerous attempts since then. In the drug scene, hardly a month goes by without some attempt to co-ordinate the agencies. I sometimes used to wonder whether anyone was actually doing any work with drug addicts, but everybody was co-ordinating the work! The workers in the West End area (who knew each other very well) were constantly being invited by officials from other bodies to come together into a co-ordinating group for the West End. We usually found that this was more for the benefit of the organization concerned, since, although we all knew each other, those who had called the meeting did not know anybody! Yet the need for co-ordination is a real one for there are a whole host of projects which fail in aim and efficiency, which bear no relationship to each other, and which seem to have sprung into existence purely on an *ad hoc* basis. The classic example of this occured soon after I had left the East End when the only two 'specialized' shelters for crude spirit alcoholics in the British Isles opened within weeks of each other, a few hundred yards apart, in Cable Street. In the drug scene too there has been a sudden growth of interest and activity, a great deal of duplication and overlapping, and a tendency for groups and organizations to answer the needs of those who founded them more than those of society as a whole.

If summer 1967 was a summer of love, it was also a summer of acid, representing the first major epidemic of LSD abuse in the United Kingdom. LSD had been introduced medically in 1954 in Britain and there had been considerable, unpublicized use of the drug in psychiatry from that time onwards. It was not, however, until 1962 that non-medical use of psychedelic drugs began in the United States, and in 1966 it played a more important role than cannabis in providing the pharmacological basis for the growth of the hippy culture in San Francisco. Out of the San Francisco area came acid rock, new experiences in psychedelic sounds as well as a whole new vocabulary, and the resulting 'psychedelic culture' made a tremendous impact throughout the nation. The writings of Timothy Leary were becoming known among a restricted audience in 1965, but it was not until 1967 that the use of LSD, and the popularizing of an Underground culture in which it played a central role, really caught on among young people. The British psychedelic movement drew considerable cultural support and inspiration from San Francisco. It was from there that the new vibrations, the emerging brotherhood of love, were seen to emanate. As one of their poets said:

> 'Oh beautiful for hairy beard,
> For psychedelic smiles,
> For strobescopes and costume weird
> And runaway juveniles.
> Haight-Ashbury, Haight-Ashbury,
> America unbound!
> Within thy good old neighbourhood
> The rising Underground.'

In June 1967 the San Francisco Deanery Clergy issued a statement:

The Church must take the hippy movement seriously . . . . These young people are saying something . . . . If the Church simply condemns the subculture for drug abuse, or for vagrancy, or for uncleanness, or for irresponsibility (whatever that may be) it falls into the position of defending intrinsic values—values which need no defending if they do indeed exist. If the Church is really to exercise its prophetic ministry, it must be open to communicate the real message of the new Haight-Ashbury community to the world, and to communicate the Gospel of Freedom to the Haight-Ashbury.

Why was LSD so important? What does it do? It is one of

the most powerful of all psychoactive chemicals and its ingestion brings about profound alterations in an individual's subjective environment with changes in perception and in consciousness. Dr Humphrey Osmond, in the earliest definition of 'psychedelic' in a paper published in 1957, described a psychedelic compound such as LSD as one which 'enriches the mind and enlarges the vision'. Because of its action the drug has been compared to mystical experience in which for a period of time the individual transcends his ego and attains a state of 'cosmic consciousness'. Timothy Leary sees the psychedelic experience as 'a journey to new realms of consciousness' in which may occur 'the transcendence of verbal concepts, of space-time dimensions, and of the ego or identity'. But there is a dark side to the picture. Many experience adverse reactions. The drug may precipitate a long-term psychological disorder of schizophrenic type. In the psychedelic community which was emerging in 1967, LSD symbolized and helped to create a new approach to reality by breaking down the walls of the ego, but it also led many into an area of consciousness where they were lost and from which they only returned as broken and disintegrated people.

The incidence of adverse reactions or 'bad trips' was so great in the San Francisco psychedelic culture that emergency medical facilities became an urgent necessity. The formation of the Haight-Ashbury Free Clinic on 7 June 1967 marked a vitally important stage in the growth of counter-culture medical care. It was the first of a number of free clinics to be set up, and in 1970 I attended the first symposium of free clinics at the University of California Medical Centre. Today in the Bay Area besides the Haight—Ashbury Clinic, there are the Black Man's Free Clinic, formed in October 1968 in McAllister Street, serving the Filmore ghetto district, and the Berkeley Free

Clinic, formed in May 1969 and closely linked with the Berkeley Free Church and with the free speech movement. There are also free clinics in Los Angeles, Seattle, Boston, Washington and New York.

The emergence of the Haight-Ashbury Free Clinic was one of the most positive and long-lasting events of the summer of 1967. Its full story and background are told by Dr David Smith, its founder, in *Love Needs Care* (1971). Initially the clinic was intended to be a 'calm centre' where bad LSD trips could be dealt with. In 1967 it was dealing with about forty bad trips a day, and throughout the summer, from July to September, about 10,000 patients were seen. In the calm centre, a quiet room with subdued lights, the patients were 'brought down' with low-pitched, positive conversation ('talkdown') with a stress on changing anxiety into a realization that they were still themselves. The clinic's methods of 'crisis intervention' and 'talkdown' are now widely used in bad trip services in this country as well as the United States.

Another characteristic feature of the period since 1967 has been the enormous volume of literature about drug abuse which has appeared in this country. In 1967 there was very little, apart from some rather technical but dated material such as E.M. Schur's *Narcotic Addiction in Britain and America,* a great deal of American material which was not applicable to the British situation, and a certain amount of hysterical and factually ill-informed literature, most of it of Christian origin, I felt that there was a need for a fairly cold, factual account of drug abuse problems which was addressed directly to adolescents. It was in an attempt to meet this need that *Drugs for Young People: Their Use and Misuse* was published in November 1967. It was written with a colleague, Brenda Jordan, and was published during the week that I began my work on the full-time staff in Soho.

On the same day as the book appeared, my first day as curate of the parish, I was summoned to the Old Bailey to give evidence for the defence in the trial of Herbert Selby's novel *Last Exit to Brooklyn*. It was a curiously symbolic beginning to a ministry in Soho. The trial attracted national publicity and brought upon me a certain amount of abuse and the usual anonymous letters. Some of the evidence for the prosecution was quite fantastic. I was asked to comment on the extent to which the book reflected accurately the social problems of city districts. I suggested that Selby had portrayed with a great deal of sensitivity some of the despair and frustration of human beings and if that helped to spread understanding and compassion among its readers, the effect could only be good. It had certainly been some help to me personally. I was asked whether I would be prepared to distribute copies around Soho. This seemed to me to be a particularly ridiculous suggestion both because the book had been published in Soho—by Calder and Boyars in Brewer Street—and was sold widely there, and also because the people of Soho were perfectly well acquainted with the issues discussed in the book. I explained that it would be preferable to distribute copies in the 'respectable' suburbs of London where people preferred to shut their eyes to the realities which the novel described.

I felt that the trial exposed two continuing characteristics of our society. The first was the widespread and deep-rooted fear of, and disgust at, sexuality and the tendency to view 'depravity' and 'corruption' in exclusively or predominantly sexual terms. It was always the descriptions of sexual intercourse, never the descriptions of violence and bloodshed, which were alleged to affect readers adversely. The second characteristic was the wide gulf between the generations and the determination of many to maintain the gulf. The *Oz* trial of 1971 brought out the same trend more clearly. My ministry in Soho began with the trial of *Last Exit* and ended with the trial of *Oz*.

So in November 1967 I became part of the full-time staff of a parish which I already knew quite well and with some of whose problems I was already heavily involved. My Rector, John Hester, was well-established in pastoral work in the theatrical world through the Actors' Church Union. He was then based at St Anne's House though he later moved his office to St Pauls' Covent Garden. Also on the full-time staff at St Anne's at this time was Miss Joan De Saumarez-Brock, a devoted and remarkable lady in her seventies, who held the post of Warden of St Anne's House and was widely known among alcoholics and vagrants in the area as 'the lady'. Judith Piepe was still officially on the part-time staff but had virtually withdrawn. Later, in 1970, we were to be joined by Susan Davis and for a time by John Hamblin.

The parish of Soho is a particularly strange one in three main respects. First, in that its pastoral involvement is more with the non-residents than with the residents, for while the residents number only a few thousand, they are heavily outnumbered by those who pour into the district by day or by night. Secondly, Soho has no Anglican parish church, and although there is a small chapel inside a large house, the pastoral ministry is far more 'dispersed' than in more conventional areas. Thus I found that I was spending more time in coffee bars, clubs, pubs and bars than in a church building, and I saw my emerging ministry as that of a 'detached priest', detached not in the sense that I was in any way separate from the Body of Christ, but certainly in the sense that I consciously severed myself from the bondage of an institution in order to be of service to a wider population. I began to find that I was moving in circles where a priest had never been seen, and spending more time with non-Christians than with Christians. It seemed to me then, as now, that the essence of priesthood lies in sacrifice and reconciliation: the priest exists to reconcile man to God and to the rest of humanity, to build bridges, to break down barriers, to lose himself in serving the world. In Soho I felt that if I could achieve anything at all, it would be through immersing myself in the subcultural life of the district, in what was popularly misnamed the 'underworld' and in identifying myself particularly with the isolated and the outcast. The *Last Exit* trial was symbolic of the world in which I was to minister: it represented the hopelessness and tragedy of so many, and the enormous gulf which is perpetuated when we shut our eyes to the sufferings of others. As one of the witnesses for the prosecution commented, with tragic irony, he did not mind such things happening in real life, but he did object to their happening in literature.

3

HUNG UP ON THE NEEDLE

When I first began to spend time around the Soho clubs in 1965 the worlds of the heroin addict or 'junkie' and of the amphetamine user or 'pillhead' were very clearly separate. The society of those who were involved with the needle was very restricted. Schur in his study of 1965 rejected the idea that there was any 'addict subculture' in Britain, and American observers were anxious to point out that British addicts were geographically dispersed, rarely in contact with each other, and predominantly middle-class. Towards the end of the 1950s, a group of Canadian heroin addicts had settled in London and many of them became the patients of a particular doctor. Some of these were responsible for infecting young English youths by selling from the surplus of their prescriptions which in most cases were large and in some cases were enormous. Probably the role of these Canadian addicts in spreading addiction has been exaggerated. But it is certainly possible to trace the early spread of a heroin subculture among the young in London, by a study of case to case infection, to the early addict society in the early 1960s. Until the end of the 1960s, however, the needle culture did not affect many working-class youths, and even as late as 1967 the teenagers who used the all-night coffee clubs in Soho were mainly involved in amphetamines taken by mouth.

The early heroin addicts used to use two pubs to the north of Oxford Street as meeting places. Boots' at Piccadilly Circus was popular for the cashing of prescriptions, and the junction of Coventry Street and Haymarket became widely known as 'junkies' corner', a reputation which it retained long after most of the addicts had left. These addicts were fairly isolated, lonely individuals. They tended to be middle-class and to be of above average intelligence. I got to know a number of these pre-1965 addicts. Brian was a middle aged Canadian who had been addicted for about twenty years. Paul was a young East Londoner who used to frequent some of the bigger West End clubs, and had been on heroin since about 1964. Keith was one of the original East End addicts. He was working-class, very out of touch with the junkie literature or with the West End bohemian/jazz/folk idiom, and he used the West End merely as a source of supply. Jean, a young South London girl, had been addicted to heroin since 1962. Many of these early addicts are now dead, many are still addicted and have a legendary status around the West End, while others are 'cured'. They were never involved as a group with the all-night club world of the adolescent pill-takers, although some of them passed through the café 'pot and pills' stage in their early days, and some of the younger ones became involved in the clubs in Soho after 1967.

I found these early junkies much easier to relate to than the younger 'teeny bopper' pillhead kids. This was partly due to my own personality: the addicts tended for the most part to be fairly introverted, meditative, dreamy people—a bit like me! But it was also because they were emotionally very dependent, rather in the way that small children or very immature teenagers are. So long as they got their heroin, they would praise you to the skies as the greatest gift to the drug scene, and they would help to inflate your ego with their plausible addict blarney. Heroin addicts are good manipulators and can put on the agony as well as the charm. The early addicts too were a fairly articulate group. Once one became known as a sympathetic counsellor, there was no great problem about being accepted within the addict subculture: the problem was rather that of how to wean addicts from oneself, in order to enable them to grow and mature.

All-night cafés, clubs and bars were sometimes harder to get into, particularly where they consisted of a tightly-knit subculture of a delinquent type. I found the Soho coffee clubs for the most part fairly easy—the management were sympathetic, and the clientele quickly accepted me as part of the scene. But there were other places where I found it hard going. One of these was a pub chiefly frequented by servicemen and other mainly middle-aged men looking for homosexual satisfaction, and by 'rent boys' and others waiting to help meet the demand and exploit them. I never really found pastoral work practicable here, although a priest who was more turned on to the gay scene might have found it easier. I always felt awkward and uncomfortable here in a way that I never did among the younger gay set. Only if I were seen as part of a well-established drinking group would I be accepted in this pub as a non-hostile presence, and even then the relationship was that of a superficial pub chat. Another difficult one was a club which was used by skinheads from all over London. Part of the problem here was that they themselves felt threatened by, and insecure in, the atmosphere of the West End, and so they built up barriers of aggression against any interlopers. Perhaps also they were less conscious of any obvious 'need', and did not take kindly to 'do-gooders'. Usually my 'method', insofar as I had one, in places which were difficult to penetrate was to go around with somebody who was accepted. This had its dangers, however, chiefly that of being identified with one clique or group. At different times I was identified closely with the male homosexual community with junkies, and with left-wing beatnik groups. One can become too worried about this danger: no priest can expect to be good with all sections of the community, and it is very important to accept one's limitations.

Sometimes it is possible to work with the individual members of a group, but never to touch the group itself as such. An example of this was Hell's Angels. I have never at any point been involved with any chapter of Hell's Angels or with Angels as a group. But individual Hell's Angels have often come through St Anne's, and I found myself involved with them frequently in discussions about magic, the occult and psycho-spiritual problems. The fact that I knew San Francisco and Oakland, even though superficially, was of great prestige value, and I was able to help individual Angels over particular problems.

Towards the end of 1967 and particularly during 1968 we were caught up in the most significant drug epidemic in the recent history of London's drug culture. Methylamphetamine hydrochloride began to circulate on a large scale, usually in the form of Methedrine ampoules. Methedrine is a very powerful cerebral stimulant and had been introduced originally in the late 1930s, its use being restricted to post-operative conditions, spinal anaesthesia, and, to some extent, abreaction in psychiatry and the treatment of obesity. The use of oral Methedrine became obsolete with that of the other amphetamines (though they continued to be prescribed) and by the time of the epidemic of illicit use, the clinical use of the injectible preparation had become very limited. Why did Methedrine use increase during 1968? I think it is clear that the activities of three doctors in particular were responsible for the spread. One doctor substituted Methedrine for cocaine as a stimulant to be used alongside heroin. So injectible Methedrine began to spread among two sections of the drug-taking population. The first was that of heroin addicts who now began to use Methedrine instead of cocaine. The second was the amphetamine users who had progressed from oral to intravenous use of the drug. It was the spread of Methedrine ampoules which, above all else, brought together the heroin addicts and the wider community of adolescents who were involved with amphetamine use. It was Methedrine use which provided the bridge between the needle culture and the kids in the clubs. It was Methedrine which played the 'escalation' role which is often, wrongly, attributed to cannabis. It was Methedrine which made the process of 'fixing' an integral part of the West End drug culture. The West End was not the same after Methedrine: it was more destructive, more hopeless, more needle-centred.

There had been major epidemics of methylamphetamine abuse in Japan in the 1940s and in the United States in the 1950s and 1960s, and today it is methylamphetamine which constitutes the major illicit substance in such high drug use areas as San Francisco. The term 'speed' was the popular term for methylamphetamine, and the slogan 'Speed Kills' was widely publicized throughout the United States in 1967 and 1968. The slogan was picked up and used by the Underground Press in Britain in 1968. So *International Times* on 9 August 1968, printed a notice:

SPEED KILLS

It is not widely known that the side effects of taking certain drugs can do as much damage as the drugs themselves. Amphetamines are not as safe as has been supposed and there is growing concern on the scene about the widespread use of methedrine.

The amphetamine methedrine is a powerful drug which distorts the mental state. Although it is used clinically to cure such disorders as Parkinsonism, Epilepsy, Enuresis and Obesity, abuse of the drug can have lasting and devastating effects.

Methedrine is one of the most dangerous drugs around at the moment and although it is less physically addictive than heroin, its prolonged use can cause very unpleasant conditions.

The most striking feature of someone who is habituated to methedrine is a paranoid psychosis with delusions and hallucinations which may be indistinguishable from paranoid schizophrenia. A methedrine user feels persecuted—friends become enemies—voices of a persecutory nature may be heard and the persecutors (real to the sufferer but totally imaginary) may be seen and attacked.

Methedrine taken for a prolonged length of time will stop a girl's periods and diminish sexual potency. There is a possibility of brain damage even after the use of the drug is discontinued and the conditions mentioned earlier can happen sooner or later to anyone who shoots methedrine.

In fact fixing any drug with unsterile needles can cause

Septicaemia (blood poisoning)
Tetanus (lockjaw)
Jaundice
Gangrene
Abscesses
Syphilis
Gonorrhoea
For further information ring Release
SPEED KILLS

The slogan was fairly successful, and Methedrine never

really caught on within the British Underground which has always remained loyal to cannabis and the psychedelics. But in 1968 Soho was a speed scene, and the damage remained long after the voluntary restriction of November 1968 by which the drug was withdrawn from retail pharmacies.

Methedrine keeps people awake for abnormally long periods of time, and so deprives the body of food and rest. We found that it was a particularly attractive drug among the young vagrants in the West End because it removed these two basic necessities of life. The immediate sensation after an injection is the 'flash' which has been described as a 'total body orgasm'. In the United States, methylamphetamine circulates in crystal form, and is illicitly manufactured in black market speed labs. Kids in such areas as Haight-Ashbury will inject 1,000—5,000 milligrammes per day, although the pharmacology textbooks say that 250 milligrammes is a lethal dose. The 'speed freak' has usually been through the stage of oral use of the drug, and his first experience of injection will be one of ecstasy. After several months he will inject the drug many times each day, and may remain awake for three to six days continuously. During this period he becomes more and more tense and paranoid, and finally 'crashes', that is, falls into a period of very deep sleep which will last for a day or more. The 'flash' and the 'crash' are the two peaks of the intravenous speed scene. There seems little doubt that short-term use of amphetamine can precipitate a paranoid psychosis in non-psychotic individuals, and large-dose amphetamine abuse appears to replicate the schizophrenic psychosis more closely than other drugs such as LSD. Out of 310 intravenous amphetamine users who sought help at the Haight-Ashbury Clinic in the summer of 1967, nearly 90 per cent showed acute anxiety reactions, nearly 60 per cent showed amphetamine psychosis, while smaller numbers were suffering from exhaustion or withdrawal.*

In 1968 the Institute of Psychiatry's Addiction Research Unit made a study of Methedrine abuse in London, and interviewed seventy-four users. Their conclusions were published in the *British Medical Journal* on 21 June 1969, and were similar to those of the American research.

In 1968 I got to know a group of lesbian Methedrine users who clustered around a set of clubs and coffee bars in the north of Soho. They constituted a tightly-knit group which was held together by the needle, by sexual relationships and by the subcultural life both of Soho and of prison. As a group, they moved between the clubs and prison with ritual rapidity. As with the young male homosexual group in the club which I described earlier, relationships in this group were pretty unstable, but they tended to last longer, and their break-ups, if they occurred, to be more tragic, than among the boys. I found these girls tremendously kind and warm, but intensely jealous and possessive.

At the same period in which I was concerned with these girls in Soho, Dr Paul D'Orban, Medical Officer of Holloway Prison, was of great help to them in the prison setting. His study of heroin dependence and delinquency in women, published in 1970 in the *British Journal of Addiction*, was based on a study of sixty-six girls, many of whom overlapped with my Soho group. His conclusions were that the girls were, on the whole, above average in intelligence but showed poor educational attainment; that most of them had a highly unstable work history prior to their addiction, and that their sources of income were precarious and often obscure. At their time of arrest, thirty-five of the sixty-six had no fixed abode or were

* The most thorough study of the San Francisco speed scene is in David E. Smith (ed), *Journal of Psychedelic Drugs, Volume Two, Issue Two: Speed Kills—A Review of Amphetamine Abuse.*

sleeping rough. There was no history of mental illness, alcoholism, drug addiction or crime in most of the families, and only a small percentage had been in psychiatric hospitals before they were addicted. But there was a high incidence of broken homes—63 per cent had suffered such deprivation under the age of fifteen, and 39 per cent under the age of five. Of the group, 48 per cent were exclusively or predominantly homosexual, and D'Orban found that 'homosexual orientation generally predated drug abuse, and did not appear to be causally related to involvement in the drug subculture'. They were a very highly disturbed group, and, viewed in the context of their general disturbance, their drug addiction seemed a minor symptom.

Both among this group of girls, and among the general community of Methedrine users, the cult of the needle was more important than the drug itself. This was true of intravenous users in general. They tended to be com pulsive drug users, and Methedrine (and other amphet-amines) was a drug which lent itself to such compulsive use, more than, for example, LSD did. This was because tolerance did not develop so quickly, and also because the amphetamines tended to relieve anxiety whereas LSD would often provoke it. The role of the needle within a group of users is central, and turning on the Methedrine almost always occurred within a group setting. Within such a group of 'speed freaks', there is compulsive talking, frenzied activity and an apparent euphoria. Hyper-activity is common. The steps of St Anne's House, regularly used for vomiting and urinating by the local alcoholics, were never scrubbed so well as in the days of Methedrine! But more important is the excessive talk. Many speed users feel that after the initial flash they can talk more easily to others about their problems, and there is often a flow of self-expression, even if nobody else is listening. Equally common is an onrush of enthusiasm, when the user may profess undying love for some other person, or may express his conversion to religion, and so on.

Getting a user off the needle is more important than getting him off the drug. It is possible for a cannabis or LSD user to make a good adjustment to life in spite of, and in a few cases because of, his drug use. But once a person is involved with the needle, he is involved in a very destructive way of life. Destructive, not simply physically in terms of overdose, infection or death, but in terms of the effect on his personality, his sexual behaviour, and his social relationships. Often the 'fix' takes the place of sexual intercourse, and one finds a lot of very disturbed sexuality within the needle culture. It has been suggested that the needle user is a chronically depressed individual who seeks to prolong an act of self-destruction, which is also a frustrated search for release. Bert Jansch's song *Needle of Death* expresses it thus:

> 'Through ages man's desire
> To free his mind, to release his very soul,
> Has proved to all who live
> That death itself is freedom for evermore,
> And your troubled young life will make
>   you turn
> To a needle of death.'

If this is so, our task is to try to help the addict to change his life-style from one which leads to death and destruction to one which leads to life and hope.

All through the period of involvement with addicts in the East End, and even more so during our early time in Soho, we were continuously conscious of the inadequate, indeed virtually non-existent, facilities for treatment. It was during 1967 and 1968 that the campaign for treatment centres became really militant. In order to relate the history of this campaign as we saw it, I need to return to my letter to *The Times* of 9 November 1966. In this letter I had referred to the Minister of Health's statement of 2 August 1966, in the Commons. In this he claimed, 'There are already centres for the treatment of addicts, and more beds could be made available if the demand increases'. (*The Times*, 3 August.) I was puzzled by this claim, which seemed to bear little relationship to the actual situation which I was encountering almost daily, and I wrote to the Ministry for clarification. In a letter dated 19 August 1966, a Ministry of Health official informed me that the Minister, in his statement, 'was not referring to any action that had been taken following the second report of the Brain Committee', but rather to 'some specialized units' which already existed. It went on: 'It may be of interest to add that there are thirty or so hospitals in the London area which accept drug addicts for treatment as in-patients including the specialized units.' But of the out-patient clinics there was no sign.

Meanwhile, doctors who had been seeing, and prescribing for, addict patients, were withdrawing from the scene. On 11 November the *Sun* devoted a good deal of its front page to an announcement that Dr Geoffrey Dymond would no longer be seeing heroin addicts. He had about eighty addicts as patients. On the same day, the *Daily Mirror* reported that addicts were calling at the Home Office for help, and claimed that one hundred and thirty addicts were affected by Dr Dymond's withdrawal. These reports were followed by longer accounts in the *Guardian* on 19 November ('Two ministries refuse to help drug addicts') and the *Sunday Times* on 20 November ('Addiction: the official double-talk, and the daily realities of treatment'). Dr Hawes was reported as having sent his applicants to the Ministry of Health. The Dymond affair sparked off a certain amount of publicity, and probably alerted the Ministry of Health to the fact that something was happening. But it was not until 1967 that the battle began in earnest.

Early in 1967 two Chelsea doctors, Peter Chapple and Geoffrey Gray, opened the Chelsea Addiction and Re search Institute (later the National Addiction and Re-search Institute) at premises in Beaufort Street. The *Sun*, in an article on 12 January, described them as 'defiant doctors . . . tired of waiting for Government action'. However, on 28 January, the *Guardian* reported informal discussions about the establishment of treatment centres. This followed the issue of a memorandum from the Ministry of Health to all the regional hospital boards, urging hospitals to collaborate in the treatment of addicts. By this time the Press was assuming that the implement-ation of the Brain proposals would take place—sometime. On 8 March, the Minister issued a memorandum suggest-ing that the London hospital boards should introduce out-patient services for heroin addicts *immediately,* and that in-patient services should be expanded, and on 25 April, during the Commons Standing Committee on the Dangerous Drugs Bill, he rejected accusations that hosp-ital facilities would be inadequate.

On 20 June, the Dangerous Drugs Bill was debated in the Lords. Lord Stonham claimed that the Bill would 'help considerably in containing the general problem and bringing compassionate but real help to those who need it' *(Hansard,* House of Lords, Volume 283, No. 163, column 1271.) He pointed out that 'addicts are free at any time to seek treatment' (column 1272), though he wisely did not say where! 'I will leave it to my noble friend Lady Phillips', he explained, 'to describe in more detail when she comes to wind up the debate our plans for a system of special treatment centres for addicts to heroin and cocaine' (column 1275). But when at last Lady Phillips rose, her contribution was, 'I was asked to tell the House something about the treatment centres. I am not certain at this stage that it would be something your Lordships would particularly wish to know.' (column 1316.)

In the meantime impatience was growing, and on 31 May, Dr Hawes had written to the Minister, pointing out that the position had changed for the worse. Lady Frankau, a very well-known physician with large numbers of addicts as patients, had died—a factor which apparently the Ministry in its planning had not anticipated!—and there were now very few doctors who were willing to accept addicts as patients. He urged the Minister to 'put into operation as an urgent measure several temporary clinics.' On 22 June, the Ministry replied, and listed a number of hospitals in London, which, they claimed, 'had already established out-patient treatment facilities for heroin addicts.' These were St Thomas's (Lambeth); Westminster; King's (St Giles); Oldchurch (Romford); Harold Wood; Whipps Cross; St Clement's, Bow; Hackney; and North Middlesex. They added that University College Hospital 'expects to start a limited service shortly', and that Charing Cross and the Maudsley might have services later. The letter pointed out that 'until hospital facilities are available generally in London it would be premature and unhelpful to addicts as a whole, to give any publicity to the units concerned'. Precisely how, without publicity, the addicts were expected to know of the existence of such centres, the letter did not explain.

Dr Hawes, anxious to discover what 'out-patient treatment facilities' actually meant, contacted all the hospitals which had been listed, and asked them to describe their facilities. The replies were extraordinary.

Westminster and Lambeth Hospitals alone accepted that they had 'treatment centres', and gave details of their opening times. Harold Wood Hospital, however, explained that 'there has been an error in the information given to you'. 'To my knowledge', wrote the hospital secretary, 'an out-patient treatment centre in respect of Drug Addiction has not been established at this hospital'. Similarly, Whipps Cross Hospital insisted that 'we have no out-patient treatment centre for treatment of drug addicts', but that they would 'deal with' addicts in casualty (as, presumably, would any casualty hospital.) Hackney Hospital said that their treatment centre was still in process of being established. St Clement's similarly said that their centre was still 'at the paper stage', and had neither staff nor other provisions. North Middlesex Hospital said that they could only deal with patients who lived in the Tottenham, Edmonton and Enfield areas, areas which were not, at this time, if at any time, known centres of heroin addicts. Oldchurch Hospital wrote that 'there is no established out-patient treatment centre for the treatment of Drug Addiction', but that the hospital could give emergency treatment only in the casualty department. King's College Hospital said that Dr Ollendorf—a well-known critic both of the Brain Report and of the Ministry of Health!—ran an out-patient clinic once a week, but that he was in the United States at the time. University College Hospital, according to a circular from the Inner London Executive Council dated 7 July, could only accept *twelve* patients, and only from the N.W.1. and W.C.1. postal districts. So much for the Ministry's 'facilities'!

The Ministry, however, not only believed in the existence of their 'facilities' but also began to use the term 'clinics' about them. On 5 July, in the Lords, Lady Phillips said proudly, 'Noble Lords will be delighted to know that there are now in operation eleven out-patient clinics in London, and plans for four other centres are under urgent discussion.' (*Hansard,* House of Lords, Volume 284, No. 172, columns 731-732.) Nobody has ever been able to discover where these clinics were. I do not believe that they existed at all. So far as one is able to tell, Lady Phillips's 'eleven out-patient clinics' must have been somehow related to the 'out-patient treatment facilities' mentioned in the Ministry's letter, which numbered nine, and most of which were non-existent. However, two days after Lady Phillips's speech, on 7 July, the *Daily Mail* and the *Sun* simultaneously discovered an actual, functioning clinic—but it was not one sponsored by the Ministry! 'Drugs clinic in station buffet', 'Doctor holds drugs clinic in a cafe' were the headlines. Dr John Petro was shown in his 'consulting room'—the tea buffet of Baker Street Underground Station. Dr Petro had previously been seeing addicts in a West End hotel. The *Daily Mail* followed its discovery by reports of delays in the Ministry's treatment plans.

It was on 8 July also that, with Dr Hawes's collaboration, I released details of his correspondence to the Press. *The Times* of that day carried a front page article quoting the letters. On 16 July the *Sunday Times* carried a lengthy article, 'The strange case of the missing treatment centres' in which the correspondence was again quoted at length. They followed this in a later issue by a disturbing piece by Alex Mitchell describing the rejection of addicts by the alleged centres. Meanwhile, Dr Petro continued to prescribe, and on 30 May the *Daily Telegraph* had drawn attention to Dr M.W. Browdy, aged eighty-two, who was practising in Shaftesbury Av., across the road from St Anne's House, and was gathering large numbers of addicts.

At the end of 1967 Dr Petro was operating from a hotel in Bayswater, and was involved in a controversial case in

Hertfordshire Quarter Sessions in which a nine-teen-year-old girl was charged with possession. As a result of the publicity, on 11 January 1968, he appeared on the David Frost Programme on television, where he was attacked and questioned by a number of well-known figures on the London drug scene. After the broadcast, he was arrested by an officer of the Drug Squad, and charged with failing to keep his Dangerous Drugs register. At Marylebone Court on 12 January, he was allowed bail. On 14 February he was fined £1,700 with £21 costs for seventeen offences. By this time, he had moved to a surgery in Stratford, East London, where he continued to see addicts and to prescribe.

It was after the arrest of Dr Petro that a group of us at St Anne's House began to wonder what further pressure could be brought to bear upon the Ministry. At this time, the Association for the Prevention of Addiction had an office in the house which was regularly visited by West End addicts, and it was decided to open an emergency clinic. The *Daily Mail* on 13 January under a heading 'Emergency drugs for Dr Petro's patients', announced that a clinic at St Anne's would remain open throughout the following weekend. Dr Petro had flown to a village in Argyll. Addicts were phoning the Home Office who could do nothing but refer them to St Anne's, an ironic comment on the Ministry of Health's claims about treatment centres. On 15 January *The Times* ran a long article in which I was quoted as saying that the clinics were 'a figment of the Ministry's imagination' and were 'semi-fictitious'. 'In London today there are only four or five such clinics, and they operate on only a fragmentary and skeleton basis. When the crisis comes—as it did this weekend—it is in other directions that the stranded addicts will turn.' Our emergency clinic was run by Ian Dunbar and dealt with about a hundred addicts. The following weekend, on 22 January, the APA held a Press conference at St Anne's at which Dr Francis Camps, Professor of Forensic Medicine at the London Hospital Medical College, called for voluntary help to establish independent drug centres, the need for which had been shown by the success of the St Anne's clinic.

The Ministry of Health continued to insist, against all the evidence, that their clinics existed, and in a statement they claimed that there were ten hospitals in the London area for the treatment of heroin and cocaine addicts as in-patients, and fourteen hospitals for the treatment of out-patients! However, a letter from the Ministry to hospital secretaries on 26 January listed only eleven hospitals, in which, it was claimed, 'out-patient treatment facilities' were available, and four where 'emergency treatment only' was available. This was an interesting letter, and began by expressing concern that 'some drug addicts have been turned away from certain hospitals in the London area'. It proceeded to give guidelines for the use of clinics and other facilities, and it included the statement: 'If an addict arrives at a time when the clinic is functioning, he should be directed to that clinic whether or not he has an appointment, and whether or not he carried a letter of reference from his local practitioner.' Four days after this letter, on 30 January, the Minister, in a Commons Written Answer, gave the same list of 'out-patient facilities' and also listed eleven hospitals at which 'in-patient treatment facilities' were provided. By this time, the Ministry had lost virtually all its credibility, and most of the people on the drug scene had ceased to take its claims seriously. In an interview on Granada TV on 12 February, the Minister attacked those who 'suggested that the treatment facilities which I announced in the House of Commons a week ago do not exist. This is quite untrue. They do exist.'

Alex Mitchell of the *Sunday Times* was not so sure. He wrote an article, 'Minister's addict clinics are just a myth' on 18 February, in which he described the results of a survey of fifteen hospitals. Mitchell showed that the chances of an addict being taken on as a patient at any of the clinics was very small. There were long waiting lists, catchment areas, inadequate staffing and facilities, and general chaos. By 16 April, when the Dangerous Drugs (Supplies to Addicts) Regulations 1968 came into effect, the situation was becoming less confused. The treatment centres at last began to assume some reality. General practitioners were forbidden to prescribe heroin and cocaine for addicts. So, over two years after the Brain Report, there was a hope that some order might come to the confused drug scene. The Methedrine crisis, however, reached its peak as the treatment centres were becoming established, and so it was not until the middle of 1969 that one began to see some pattern emerging.

Would the clinics have appeared when they did if there had not been so much publicity? It is hard to answer. I certainly got the impression in 1967 that the attitude of the Ministry of Health was twofold. First, they condemned those wicked, over-prescribing doctors. But, secondly, they hoped that these same doctors would continue to prop up the old system until the Ministry was ready with its new treatment centres, and would then gracefully withdraw. Lady Frankau's death took them by surprise, and it led to Dr Hawes's unexpected revelations in the Press, and so brought the whole terrible business out into the open. Even then, it took a lot of publicity and publicly fought battles to force the Ministry into action. Mr Kenneth Robinson, then Minister of Health, in his television appearance on 12 February 1968, commented about the voluntary bodies, 'I only wish they found it possible to call attention to their own efforts without constantly denigrating the efforts of others, particularly the efforts of the Government, and I would have thought that at least the reverend gentlemen that are associated with these bodies would have heard of the injunction to do good by stealth'—an injunction which he presumably thought was in the Bible! This, of course, was simply a contemporary version of the advice given by Amaziah to the prophet Amos to go and work in the land of Judah, and not to prophesy at Bethel which was the seat of government (Amos 7.13). The provision of treatment facilities, like so many other forms of social care, only came as a result of an intensive campaign by voluntary agencies, much of it in the face of strong resistance.

On the day that the Dangerous Drugs Regulations made it an offence for general practitioners to prescribe heroin and cocaine for addicts, Dr Christopher Swan set up the 'East London Addiction Centre' in Queensbridge Road, Shoreditch. Its notepaper described Dr Swan as the Medical Director, while the 'Medical Secretary' was one 'Stephen Hartford (General Secretary, National Association on Drug Addiction)'. During the summer of 1968, large numbers of young pill-takers found their way to Dr Swan's clinic. On 10 January 1969, he was sentenced to fifteen years' imprisonment. John Petro, who had been struck off the Medical Register in May 1968 continued to prescribe until the end of that year, when his appeal was rejected. Later, he went on ministering informally around Piccadilly, dealing with abscesses and overdoses, and giving medical attention and advice. He was, and still is, widely respected and liked by many junkies, and many more have a kind of love-hate relationship with him. The publicity which attended these two doctors led many people to two false beliefs. The first was that these were the only, or the worst, examples of irresponsible prescribing. This is, I think, open to considerable doubt: there were others who managed to escape publicity. The second false belief was that it was the 'junkies' doctors' who were responsible for the spread of addiction. That they contributed to the drug scene is beyond dispute, but they were symptoms of a disease, not the causes of it. They were products of the so-called 'British system', a 'system' which, by 1968, for a variety of reasons, had got out of control.

During 1969 and 1970, after the Act came into operation, and the treatment centres started to function, our most serious problems of drug abuse in Soho were connected with the intravenous use of methadone (also referred to by its British trade name Physeptone) and crushed barbiturate capsules. The restrictions on Methedrine in October 1968 and the gradual reduction in supplies of heroin from this period onwards led to a search for injectible substitutes. The barbiturates, in the form of such capsules as Tuinal and Nembutal, were readily available and, when used intravenously, highly dangerous. The effect of the barbiturate drugs is to depress the central nervous system, to reduce inhibitions, and to allow the expression of conflict. Thus the barbiturate addicts, unlike heroin addicts, are often irritable, aggressive and violent. The majority of barbiturate users in the British Isles are, of course, middle-aged and elderly people, who use them, under medical direction, as sleeping agents. During 1969-70 we increasingly saw numbers of young barbiturate addicts. On 24 June 1970, the main Christian groups working in the field met at St Anne's. There were representatives of the Coke Hole Trust, the New Life Foundation, Life for the World, Hill Farm, and Spelthorne St Mary. From this meeting we sent a letter to the Home Secretary, in which we expressed concern 'that a good deal of our work is being undermined by what appears to be thoughtless, and at times irresponsible, prescribing of sedative and hypnotic drugs, particularly barbiturates, by some general practitioners. It is extremely easy in many cases for addicts to persuade doctors to prescribe barbiturates'. We suggested the introduction of a *coloured* prescription pad on which all scheduled drugs should be prescribed, and which should be kept always under lock and key or on the doctor's person.

Earlier, on 26 March 1969, Norman Fowler had reported in *The Times* another significant development, the appearance of illegally imported heroin from the Far East on the London black market. The report did not mention the Gerrard Street area of Soho, but it was well-known that this was where the illicit material was available. It was usually a mixture of heroin and caffeine, originated in Hong Kong, and sold in London at about thirty shillings (£1.50) a grain, although the actual heroin content was dubious. Within a few weeks, other reports began to appear. Alan Bestic, writing in the *Daily Mirror,* claimed that 'a highly organized trade in Chinese heroin is sabotaging the Government's year-old plan to curb Britain's epidemic of addiction'. He suggested that about five pounds of heroin was being smuggled in each month. Bestic named Gerrard Street as the centre of the 'big business' which had developed. Similar accounts, based apparently on identical sources, appeared in both *The Times* and the *Guardian* on 8 July. Analysis of 'Chinese heroin' at this time revealed that it consisted of 40 per cent heroin, 35 per cent quinine, 20 per cent caffeine, and 5 per cent of unidentified substances. This was similar to the 'Red Chicken' which was sold in Hong Kong. The traffic was in fact organized by Hong Kong expatriates, although English addicts were used to distribute to the customer. The distribution centres included Gerrard

Street and Macclesfield Street, and also the district around Goodge Street Station and Tottenham Court Road.

The physical and mental deterioration of the West End street addict was a source of concern to all the agencies working in the area. The Association for the Prevention of Addiction opened a day centre in the area, first at St Anne's House, and later at premises in Covent Garden. Later other day centres were set up, one by New Horizon, also originally at St Anne's, and then in the Drury Lane area, and another by the Helping Hand organization at Charing Cross. The APA's King Street Day Centre, which closed in 1970, had catered for the vagrant and semi-vagrant 'Piccadilly junkie'. It was a referral base, linking the addict with his clinic and with accommodation. First aid was provided for abscesses and overdoses. During 1969 the centre was seeing between forty and fifty addicts each day. Many of these were injecting barbiturates. The centre was able to provide food and nutrition, clothes, accommodation, medical and psychiatric help, and legal assistance where necessary, and to give assistance with methods of hygiene and injection. Physical assistance was the first priority, and the hard-core addict was their primary concern.

I believe that a properly run day centre is a necessary part of any care of addicts within a community such as the West End. But it needs to be seen as part of the therapeutic process, and related to an ongoing treatment programme, and to other facilities within the area. If this is not so, the day centre may become a centre for the reinforcement and spread of the needle culture and its destructive characteristics. We have found in the past at St Anne's House that by allowing addicts to gather, we were providing a base for the addict society and therefore indirectly for the spread of addiction. It is difficult sometimes to decide whether one is caring for the addict as a person or merely propping up his way of life.

We were finding that we needed to pay far more attention to after-care, and we began to act as a liaison point between the Soho street addict and therapeutic communities in other parts of the country. After-care facilities are still very poor, and in 1968 they were even worse. The Government's Advisory Committee Report *The Rehabilitation of Drug Addicts,* published in 1968, has led to very few results. It is incredibly difficult to find people and places to which former drug users can go and receive care and guidance after they have left hospital. It is partly because of this that relapse to drugs occurs so frequently. But even where attempts at after-care are made, relapse is still common, and one has to be prepared for continual failures and be ready to start afresh. Thus Violet, a girl who had been on heroin in the early 1960s, nearly died during the vicious winter of 1967-68. She was admitted to a succession of hospitals, and finally we got her away from London to a family in the West of England. After several moves around the country, during which she moved in and out of hospitals, she returned to Soho after an absence of three years. What will become of her now one does not know, but she has brought at least eight people to the point of nervous exhaustion through her immaturity and dependence. Again, Mary was a young girl who originally started to use amphetamines in a café in a northern city, and after a period in approved schools and borstals, she hit Soho in 1967, when she began to use heroin. She developed a lesbian relationship with a girl whom she had met in Holloway, and together they returned to the north. But after six months the attraction of Piccadilly was too great, and she returned and became a dealer in illicit heroin. In spite of various attempts at after-care, she always returns to Soho where her physical condition quickly deteriorates. There are many other examples. It is important to continue to hold them in prayer and not to lose hope even where the future seems very bleak indeed.

On the other hand, it is not correct to say, as many do, that no drug addicts are ever 'cured'. Jack lived a vagrant life around Piccadilly, sleeping in St Martin's Crypt in the daytime and hanging around an all-night coffee-bar in St Anne's Court at night. He was using heroin and crushed barbiturate capsules. In 1969 we were able to find him a place in an agricultural community in the West of England, and, after considerable guidance and care, he married, and has now been off all drugs for over two years. Roy and Karen were both addicted to heroin, and, through the care of an evangelical group in the South of England, are now off, have a small baby, and are growing spiritually in a marvellous way. Jackie was part of the lesbian community in Soho and used Methedrine, but was never heavily involved with the needle. We placed her with a family outside London, from whom, after some months, she ran away, and was arrested and charged with theft of a vehicle. After a return to prison, we lost contact with her until she turned up on a farm in the West country where for two years now she has been in charge of the poultry. In all these cases, however, a tremendous amount of time, patience and love has been required.

A very large part of our work in Soho has been with young people for whom, at present at any rate, the West End of London is an integral part of their life-style. Hence our ministry has not been one of after-care or 'rehabilitation' but simply of containment. We have tried to provide crisis caring within this area of high infection. There are a large number of young drifters who move between Soho and the problem districts of other cities and towns, and are known to most social workers, probation officers and clergy in all these places. The most extreme example of this pattern is a young man, Geordie, who must be known to every social agency between Land's End and John O' Groats. On one occasion a London probation officer compiled a list of twenty-nine social workers and others in London who were *currently* involved with his problems! In a short period, I have had telephone calls or letters about him from a social worker in Liverpool, Samaritans and a Methodist church in Manchester, prison chaplains in Wakefield, Liverpool, Durham and London, and a Franciscan friar on his way to Inverness! He moves about the country at an incredible speed, collects social workers and clergymen as others collect stamps, but always returns to Soho and to the bars around Piccadilly. The West End can contain him while other areas of the country find him quite impossibly deviant in his behaviour and manner, and he invariably gets into trouble when he leaves Soho for long. There are many young people who would be labelled 'psychopaths' or 'psychotic' for whom the West End is a magnet: within its subcultural life, they can lose themselves for a time. It is important therefore to see that all the forces which operate within the West End scene are not destructive and negative in their impact upon such individuals. Part of our ministry at St Anne's has been to provide what the Americans would call crisis intervention facilities.

NOTE. The names of drug users and former drug users mentioned here have all been altered, and in some cases other aspects of their identity had been disguised.

4

YOUTH ON THE DRIFT

It would be completely wrong to view the West End of London solely in terms of drug use. Drugs attract the publicity, and people outside Soho often assume that our entire work was drug-orientated. In fact, drug problems represent only one facet of an evolving youth culture. In the West End district, in fact, a number of distinct cultures co-existed. My friend and former colleague, Rod Moore, who used to be on the staff of the Rink Project, suggested that there were three major strands of West End youth. First, the 'club culture', concentrated on the all-night clubs, mainly to the north of Shaftesbury Avenue (with the exception of the Gerrard Street district). Secondly, the young vagrant community around Covent Garden, Charing Cross and Piccadilly, extending into some of the Soho coffee bars and amusement arcades. Thirdly, what Rod called 'an area of idealization and rationalization', represented by a more consciously 'drop-out' group who would articulate their life-style in language derived from Marcuse, from leaders of student revolt, and the politics of alienation. Those who were involved in work with 'unattached youth' in the West End tried to divide our areas of concern so that there was not too much overlap, and we were able to focus on particular areas. So, during 1968-70, I tended to concentrate on the clubs and coffee bars, while Alistair Cox, Rod Moore, and their colleagues were mainly concerned with the young vagrant community, and Phil Cohen (who, as 'Dr John', led the sit-ins at Broad Court and 144 Piccadilly in 1969) was involved with the activist 'street commune' group.

The small clubs in Soho consist usually of a basement room with a juke box, fruit and football machines, and a bar which sells Pepsi and orange drinks and coffee. The kids who use these clubs include both 'week-enders'—fairly ordinary non-delinquent or 'fringe' delinquent youngsters from most parts of Greater London—and the hard core of disturbed youngsters for whom the West End is 'home', if anywhere is. It is this group with which we have been very much involved pastorally. They were all drug users, many of them were involved with homosexual or 'straight' (heterosexual) prostitution and most of them were former inmates of prisons or borstals. They belong to the club world as to a village, and they move along a regular sad circuit from one club to another. The Soho clubs run on circuits. Thus a small group of clubs in one district might attract the same groups of youngsters at different periods of the night. There were exceptions: for example, one club consisted solidly of black kids who would not frequent the other clubs in the vicinity to the same extent. The young 'gay' (homo-sexual) boys' club was on a different circuit, which included clubs in Earl's Court and the King's Road area of Chelsea. But on the whole the little group of clubs in the northern part of Soho catered for a common population. I found that if I stayed in one club for half of the night, I would meet a very large cross-section of this population The managements were very cooperative, and at times helpful, and so I and other workers were always admitted to these clubs free of charge.

In the early stages of the work I thought that a clerical collar would be a disadvantage and would inhibit contact. however, I felt that the possible snags were counter-balanced by the need to get known quickly. I soon found that it was a distinct advantage to be seen as a priest. First, because it meant that one became known and identifiable over a very wide area quickly, and many kids whom I did not know would recognize me at a later date. Secondly, because it was the surest way not to be mistaken for a plain-clothes policeman, a danger which many youth workers have had to face. But, thirdly, I found that, far from inhibiting, the presence of a priest in the club had exactly the opposite effect. The usual opening line was, ''Ere, you ain't a vicar, are you?' This might be followed up by attempts to shock, 'dirty' jokes and 'mickey taking'. These were a terrific help because they enabled me to establish friendships and break down barriers and they also shattered whatever might still remain in me of the 'respectable clergyman' image. There were some memorable comments. ''E ain't no bleeding vicar', sneered a young man in an audience at a youth club in Barnet, 'I've seen 'im down the Flamingo'. In the Alphabet Club in Gerrard Street, a girl walked past me in the dark, then swung around and stared, and finally, with a look of relief, said, 'Blimey, for a minute I thought you was a vicar!' contacts made in the clubs would often present themselves years later. I met a young man in Haight-Ashbury, San Francisco, who had last met me in a Soho club. Frequently I have met kids in other parts of Britain whom I originally met in Soho.

The value of making contacts in the clubs, of course, is that you are meeting young people on their own ground. You are not protected by a church, you are exposed to criticism, anger and aggression, and people are free to treat you as they wish. The danger is that you are intruding where you are not wanted, and if the freedom of young people is not respected, club visiting can easily become a form of 'do-goodery', rather condescending 'missionary work' which is strongly, and rightly, resented.

The kids in the clubs loathe the crusaders who come to the clubs in order to convert, rescue and save them from the wickedness of Soho. One has to tread carefully, as well as prayerfully, here. So much harm has been done by individuals who have been attracted by the notoriety of Soho, and have seen the clubs as happy hunting grounds for their zeal. We were very conscious that we were inheriting a lot of the hostility and suspicion which they had aroused. For nearly a year I used to sit drinking coffee, deliberately not speaking to people unless they spoke first, and simply trying to become part of the scenery. Once one is accepted as a trustworthy and reliable person, there are endless possibilities and ways of helping which may arise. But one needs first to establish one's role. For the Christian, this is to carry the love of Christ in one's humanity and by one's presence to enable others to feel his care for them. This is as often achieved in silence as in much speaking.

I referred above to inherited hostility and suspicion. But this is widespread and pervasive and obviously extends well beyond the limits of the Soho clubs. What kind of feelings did I arouse there? First, a certain amount of suspicion of my motives. Why was I there? What was I up to? Many people assumed that there must be some ulterior motive, some need in me which propelled me to the shadier clubs at the darkest hours. 'You must be kinky', one lad told me, 'or you wouldn't go on working here.' Was I a voyeur, a lonely homosexual, a 'grass' (police informer), a drug pusher, or just a naive, well-meaning do-gooder? All these labels were fixed on me. Secondly, there was a feeling of being 'got at', a sense that I must be there in some moralizing and condemnatory role, that I did not, could not, approve of the places, and had therefore come to rescue people from them. Thirdly, there were often feelings of anger against priests and the church, and my presence and the dog-collar evoked memories and detailed accounts of bad experiences at the hands of clergy and churches.

It is necessary not to try to ward off these feelings, but to accept them and absorb them. One can only overcome this hostility and alienation by a growing love and trust. One cannot overcome in one night the accumulated damage of many centuries of churchiness. There is a real danger, however, that one may become over-anxious and assume a 'hearty' or falsely 'with it' extrovert role. This is without doubt the surest and swiftest way to lose respect and one has seen many young well-meaning clergy who have become figures of ridicule among young people because of what they interpret as an assumed 'with-it-ness' which smacks to them of the phoney. It is possible to increase the hostility by excessive talk. Clergy talk too much anyway and we often tend to talk *at* people rather than *to* them. There is something really horrible about the clerical voice and approach which often puts people off at once, a sense that people are being seen as victims and are there to be talked down to. I am sure that unless you are a very eccentric extrovert figure (who can get away with anything) it is better to err on the side of silence.

I am a fairly shy person and I therefore found it easier to 'slide' into a coffee bar or club and be absorbed into its milieu without attracting too much attention. This I found paid off in the sense that the more isolated and distressed people would often make their way to me and talk. We need to remember that the dog-collar can be a hindrance to the very people for whom it is necessary: those who are in serious trouble and need to recognize a source of possible help through some visible mark. Yet it still requires a fair amount of courage for a young person to be seen talking with a priest, and it is important to make his path as easy as possible. Again, one should not become over-anxious or too serious about this. For many of the kids in the West End, to talk to a priest—and to 'take the mickey' out of him—was a big laugh, better than talking to a 'fuzz', and it is amazing how much serious talk you can have when you don't take yourself too seriously.

I did feel very often that I was looked upon by young people as a clerical freak, an oddity, and it was taken for granted that for a priest to be in a coffee bar, even at the fairly early hour of 11.00 p.m. was pretty unusual. The image of the conventional clergyman with his sober black suit, keeping respectable hours in respectable company, and carefully avoiding all situations of danger, dies hard. Unfortunately it has too much truth in it to be easily destroyed. The kids in the clubs may have felt embarrassed that I was 'their' priest, but they also felt that I was out on a limb, that the Church as a whole remained far removed from their world, and that to most church people, clergy or laity, they were unacceptable company.

One area in which a large part of my ministry was spent was the homosexual societies. The West End homosexual world is complex in structure. There is a fairly sharp division between the older, pre-war gay bars and clubs, where women are conspicuously absent, mistrusted and sometimes feared, and the younger gay coffee-clubs where it is unusual not to see some 'straight', as well as some lesbian, girls. From about 1969 onwards there has been a very marked shift away from Soho among the younger gay crowd, and new clubs have been springing up in Earl's Court, Kensington and Chelsea. The young homosexual in Soho almost always comes in from elsewhere and rarely lives in the West End. He finds in the West End three areas of social life. First, the exclusively gay clubs which form part of a network and are known and publicised internationally on the homosexual circuit. Secondly, a group of clubs peculiar to Soho, containing a more delinquent population, including a large number of homosexuals, some of whom are involved with prostitution or with drug abuse. Thirdly, the amusement arcades, bars, public lavatories ('cottages') and other locations near Piccadilly, where the 'rent boys' or homosexual prostitutes form a sad, but growing, group.

The West End is more criminalized than most other districts frequented by male homosexuals. The two most famous homosexual pubs in the West End are dangerous and contain many 'rent boys', and this is true also of some of the drinking clubs. The young homosexual who arrives on the West End scene early, as a 'chicken', only usually stays there if he fails to mature. In the world of the coffee clubs, there is a culture with its own language, and words like bona (good), varda (to look), nishta and nanty (no) are used extravagantly. The homosexual language is called Polari, and should be distinguished from Camp language, which is more widely used and less restricted. Also today the homosexual language is becoming confused with the language of the drug culture and of the hippy scene.

Pastoral care of young homosexuals inevitably occupied a good deal of our time in Soho. I believe that we need to be far more honest in our approach to homosexuality. It is quite false to see homosexuals as a sick, disturbed minority. There are disturbed homosexuals as well as disturbed heterosexuals. But there is no doubt that social pressures have helped to make homosexual problems a major element in psychological illness. The clergy, I feel, should be more sympathetic and understanding in this field, if only because it is well known that some of our best and most respected clergy are homosexual. But it is also true that mental illness among clergy reveals homosexual problems as a significant factor. Dr Frank Lake's study of 100 clergy patients showed the 37 had homosexual experience, and an additional 37 admitted to persistent sexual phantasies. In a paper published in the *British Journal of Psychiatry* in 1969, three doctors studied 51 clergy patients and showed that sexual deviations occurred in 21.6 per cent of them. They recommended that more attention should be paid in theological training to help ordinands gain more insight into themselves and their own psychopathology. Certainly this would help clergy not only to face their own inner selves, but also to help others in the different areas of sexuality, where, all too often at present, clergy seem to be uncomfortable and repressed.

During 1970 those who were working in the field of sexual problems in London became increasingly involved with the phenomenon of transexualism. Transexuals are individuals who are born with the body of one sex but who at some stage in their lives come to identify psychologically with the other sex. They are often described by the innaccurate and misleading term 'transvestites' and, even more mistakenly, categorized as homosexuals. The first widely publicised transexual was George Jergensen, who underwent surgery in Denmark in 1953. So far little work has been done in this country on the problems of the transexual, but a good deal has been done in the United States, and in 1970 I was able to visit a number of groups and individuals there who were involved with transexual counselling. They included Zelda Suplee who works for the Erikson Foundation in New York, an educational body which with the Albany Trust had sponsored an international symposium on Gender Identity in July 1969. In San Francisco, a police officer—cum—counsellor, Elliot Blackstone of the Community Relations Division, runs an efficient counselling centre on Third Street and is involved with homophile groups all over the Bay Area. The Centre for Special Problems in Van Ness Street, San Francisco, was also seeing large numbers of transexuals and administering estrogen therapy. Estrogen is the primary female hormone, and injections of it will reduce the primary male hormone in transexuals who are biologically male. They will then develop female characteristics such as breasts and wider hips, their body hair will decrease, and libido will be reduced. The Centre found that out of 75 transexual patients seen there in one year, only one was a female-to-male. Curiously, most of the transexuals whom I have encountered in Soho have been female-to-male, and have sought surgery in order to adopt a male role.

A very different world is that of the folk clubs. I was first introduced to the contemporary folk clubs of the West End in the early 1960s by Judith Piepe. In 1965 Paul Simon paid his first visit to England and sang at the Flamingo Club in Wardour Street. Judith met him, and as a result of this encounter she recorded a series of talks on the BBC Five to Ten programme during Holy Week 1965, in which she took one of Paul's songs as a theme each day. These songs provided the basis of The Paul Simon Song Book which was issued as an LP later that year. Judith wrote a preface to the booklet version in which she said:

> Paul Simon's songs are personal and individual, the expression of his own thoughts and feelings, but in writing them he expresses the thoughts and feelings, hopes and fears, problems and frustrations, of our time, of his generation. In speaking for his generation he says what others feel but cannot find the words to say, and in doing so has a liberating and healing effect.

Earlier Paul Simon and Art Garfunkel had produced an LP in the United States, Wednesday Morning 3.A.M., which was not issued in Britain until several years later after their

songs had become famous. Paul and Art had a close
association with Soho and with St Anne's, and sang at the
Open Air Mass on St Anne's Day in 1965. Paul Simon
seems to me to represent the alienation of many young
people from organized religion and the search of many
young people for authentic spirituality. In his song
Blessed—written in St Anne's—he expressed some of his
own isolation.

> Blessed is the land and the kingdom.
> Blessed is the man whose soul belongs too.
>> Blessed are the meth drinkers,
>>> pot sellers,
>>> illusion dwellers.
>> O Lord, why have you forsaken me?

In *Sounds of Silence* which (in the appalling version sung
by The Bachelors) topped the hit parade, he sings of what
theologians call 'the problem of communication' in the
technocratic age.

> And the people bowed and prayed
> To a neon god they made,
> And the sign flashed forth its warning
> In the words that it was forming.
> And the sign said, 'The words of the prophets
>> are written on the subway walls,
>>> And tenement halls,
> And whispered in the sounds of silence'.

Songs of this type, about loneliness, rejection, brotherhood, inhumanity, were sung around the Soho folk cellars
in 1965 and 1966. Paul Simon's songs were typical of
them, and were among the best examples of them.

Another singer who used to have close links with us and

has since become famous is Al Stewart. He wrote two important songs of social protest which he sang widely in 1966. One was *Pretty Golden Hair,* a lament about the suicide of a young homosexual, which Al used to sing in the Soho clubs. The other was *Who killed Tommy McGeechy?,* the story of a Stepney meths drinker's death (an incident which also received mention in Sally Trench's *Bury Me In My Boots*). The early folk scene, however, mirrored the problems of Soho and the world. The singers were for the most part only peripherally, if at all, involved in the issues about which they sang, and the clientele in the clubs too was a mixed body of students, folk enthusiasts, and Soho regulars. But the clubs provided a kind of running commentary on the wider West End culture of which they were a small part. As the folk scene developed, it became, like its figurehead Bob Dylan, less concerned with old-fashioned protest songs, and more surrealistic, psychedelic and concerned with the inner world.

During 1968 I became friendly with Chris Simpson, now the lead guitarist and vocalist of Magna Carta. Chris was a theological student at King's College, London, and dropped out of ordination into pop music. Magna Carta, who produced their first LP soon after they had performed at St Anne's Day in 1969, have been described as England's answer to Simon and Garfunkel. Their songs are profound and beautiful mediations on twentieth century decadence. Chris and I have worked together on various ideas about religion and pop culture. The incident that sticks most in my mind was a duologue, with words and music, which we did before an audience of moral welfare workers at Swanwick in 1970. Like Paul Simon, Chris Simpson expresses in words and music the spiritual questionings of many of his generation.

Towards the end of 1968 a movement began to take

shape among a section of Piccadilly beats called 'The Commune of the Streets'. The Commune really grew out of a sit-in at the Pronto Bar in Piccadilly Circus on 9-10 November 1968, as a result of which four kids appeared in Bow Street Court on 27 November. Two days later three other members of the group appeared as a result of disturbances at Eros in October, and on 10 December a group was charged with obstruction in Playland, an amusement arcade near to the Pronto Bar. A few days before the case was heard, two committees were set up, a steering committee and a 'direct action' committee. This was the first sign of plans for direct action by the young people around Piccadilly Circus. The Commune had in mind the organization of sit-ins and boycotts against selected cafés and pubs which refused to serve beats, and the provision of 'street guides' and observers of police activity. They also announced plans for a 'beat community centre', with about twenty-five people in residence, with a street newspaper, a poster and music workshop, and a research group, as well as dossing and eating facilities for beats in London. 'The aim in getting a place', said the Commune in a bulletin of 21 November 1968, 'is not to get us off the streets which is what the straights want, but to establish a base from which we can develop a more effective way to control the streets.' The formation of the Commune was reported in the *Daily Telegraph*, and *Peace News*, and *International Times* described the Pronto Bar sit-in. Special cards and badges were announced, and membership of the Commune was to be restricted to those who were under twenty-five or felt it, had left school at sixteen or dropped out of college, and had 'no permanent/straight job or other independent means'.

Most of the Commune's plans never came to anything. Their broadsheets were filled with outlines and programmes for workshops, and extremely detailed descriptions of new magazines which were always about to appear. Thus *King Mob Echo 2* would describe 'the English Beats' seen as 'a subcultural front against straight society'. This issue was to contain an analysis of 'English Beats and the Subcultural Revolution', as well as studies of life on the road, prose, poems, songs, and 'a programme for anti-workers' control of the streets'. Later, another broadsheet announced the imminent publication of *Street Voice*—'a new fortnightly newspaper produced by the Commune of the Streets'. *Street Voice* was to be 'an instrument of action . . . forging links at street level, between the major subcultural groupings which have already invested the significant points of discontinuity in the process of socialization, in order to construct a united front, a new anti-working class, capable of detonating the key contradictions in the social structure and blockading straight society into a state of callapse.' It was to be a local newspaper for the Piccadilly area, and a pilot issue was to appear in April 1969. Needless to say, it never did appear! *Agro,* however, did manage to appear in December 1969—a pilot issue—but never appeared again. *Klap* (in which I was involved) also ran for one issue in July 1970. In 1970 also came announcements of the Muggins Trust and of Street Bond, which changed its name to Street Aid in December 1970. Finally, in 1971 yet another 'voice of the West End community', *Rubber Duck,* was published. The jargon and the style were identical with the broadsheets of 1968.

But the Commune was more significant than its abortive literature. What did it aim to do? In the original broadsheet of November 1968, the philosophy of the Commune was expressed as follows:

We are the victims of discrimination—by the police—by

the cafes and bars around Piccadilly. Tonight we have occupied the Pronto Bar (next to London Pavilion) to demand equal rights. Before you judge us, come and hear us—on the steps of Eros—in the Haymarket Arcade now!

They call us Beats. Perhaps they think they have got us beaten. They are wrong. Today our faces are painted because like our brothers in the ghettoes of Brixton and Notting Hill we are protesting against a vicious policy of social discrimination.

The Commune called for the liberation of Eros.

This is what Eros should, could be: an open forum, an academie in the real sense where people can meet and talk and dance and play at reconstructing the basis of everyday life. But thanks to police paranoia all we have got is desolation row. Thanatos suppressing Eros. Tonight we are attempting to reverse this. Eros will be reconstructed. Nameless wildness will emerge from the underground (at last). So come and join us.

At the same time, the Commune began to look for property for a base in London, and it was at this point that they became national news. In August 1969 some members of the Commune squatted in a house in Broad Court, Covent Garden. The property belonged to Charing Cross Hospital, and when, after a court injunction, they were evicted, they moved to a disused school in nearby Endell Street. Here they set up barricades, and there was water and electricity. A poster workshop was set up in the basement, and there was a street theatre group. In fact, Endell Street was kept together well, unlike Broad Court which had become very overcrowded. But in order to prevent further overcrowding and deterioration, some members of the Commune began to look around for another place, and they chose the house which soon became famous as a 'hippy stronghold'—144 Piccadilly.

My first involvement with 144 was on 3 September 1968, when three members of the Commune, Bernard, Bennett and Pete, called to see me at St Anne's House, and said that they had occupied 144 Piccadilly in the name of the 'London Arts Commune'. They asked me if I would visit the house and write a letter verifying that they were in possession. This I did on the same date. A few days later the occupation hit the national press. About fifty people had moved in initially on a Sunday evening, getting in through the basement, and they rigged up a kind of moat, a gap between the house and the street. A security group kept out invaders. One of the Commune described what happened next.

Next morning we put out banners saying we were squatting and the next thing we knew we were in the papers. Then a crowd started gathering and a load of anarchists and the usual power freaks came down hoping to start the revolution of something, you know. So we thought we'd better decide what to do, but there were so many people that nobody could agree on anything. One thing that was decided, however, was that a defence force should be formed. Somebody had invited a load of Hell's Angels down from the South Coast and Windsor Chapter, and they acted as the defence force against the police and the skinheads who had turned up for the agro. As the week went by more and more straight people were gathering outside, along with the reporters and so on. We had to vet people as they came in, to check that they weren't plain-clothes policemen or the Press. Everything was in a bit of a turmoil, what with people trying to become leaders and trying to organize food and so on. Then things like batches of cigarettes started appearing from somewhere and Apple Records gave us some Beatles' records and a record player appeared and there was quite a lot of money there. By this time there were about 5-600 people there.

After a few days, large numbers of skinheads appeared, as well as police. Plastic balls filled with water were used to throw at both skinheads and police. I still have two of these balls which were brought to me after the events. Eventually, however, the police managed to get into the house, and Phil Cohen ('Dr John') was taken to West End Central Police Station. While the 144 events were happening, the school in Endell Street was still occupied, but soon afterwards the police invaded these premises also and took away about sixty people. Most of them were given conditional discharges or suspended sentences.

The reaction of the straight press to the occupations was fairly uniformly hostile. The *Church Times* was horrified, and exclaimed, in its issue of 26 September:

Sympathy with these young anarchists is misplaced . . . Most of them seem to be simply idlers who expect to live at the expense of other people, who batten on the very society which they condemn and attack, and who are only too eager to follow the lead of a handful of ruthless men with the avowed aim of destroying the whole fabric of society.

With these sentiments the beats of Piccadilly agreed. As the writer quoted above said:

Looking back on it, I think a lot of people got the wrong idea about the Street Commune. It wasn't for squatting homeless families—in fact the whole thing was supposed to be against the family. The commune was for kids on the Dilly, kids on the road, coming into London. Some people did have political reasons for doing it, but most of the so-called politicos who came in to 144 and afterwards were too straight, they didn't understand the scene, they couldn't relate to the kids and people resented them. I think as far as most of the kids were concerned, the main reason for squatting was to get a place to stay and to get a real scene together.

At the end of 1969 the pilot—and only!—issue of *Agro* tried to mobilize skinhead opinion. The paper ('printed by the Gutter Press'), bore the stamp of the Commune and most of it in fact consisted of an abridged version of 'Project Free London', a small booklet to which I shall refer again. The Editorial claimed that *Agro* would be produced and distributed, not from an office, but through an informal network of 'skinheads, greasers, heads; in pubs, caffs, clubs and on the streets'. The Commune was worried because skinheads and greasers had mobilized against each other instead of against straight society, and they saw *Agro* as a way of combining forces as a 'single subcultural front'. Again, there were extravagant promises of articles, there was to be a skinhead section containing a special report on the East End Scene, a greaser section with a discussion by teds, greasers and angels on changes in their scene, a heads section, a skoll section (the Free Underground Campaign for Kids), and so on. In fact, nothing happened.

The most curious events of all occurred in Summer 1970 when a strange alliance between the Salvation Army and indirectly) the Commune produced the West End Summer Programme, a largely abortive project of which I was chairman. Rod Moore of the Rink Project felt strongly that something should be attempted for the benefit of the 'summer youngsters' who usually flooded the West End in the summer months of each year. The majority of these youngsters stayed around for a limited period and were fairly average, adventurous young people for whom the West End offered a limited experience of freedom. The original idea of the Summer Programme was to provide two or three workers from the Rink Project, a detached work project sponsored by the Salvation Army, to observe and participate in this 'summer scene', to liaise with other bodies who were involved with these new-comers, and to interpret the significance of the events to official agencies. We did not see the Programme in 'problem' terms, but rather as a means of contact and information. We felt that a newspaper would be the most effective way of maintaining a regular commentary on the events of the summer.

The project was not a success, partly because the expected summer influx did not occur, and partly because of a breakdown in communication between the conventional social workers, clergy and youth workers, and the kids on the Dilly who were producing the paper. The beats associated with the Commune, including Phil Cohen who by 1970 had been taken over by the Soho Project, exhibited aggression and mistrust towards 'social workers' whom they saw as reformists and stooges of the establishment. The more 'established' agencies saw the Commune as thoroughly irresponsible. All in all the Summer Programme was a fiasco. But out of the salvage emerged Street Aid, the first welfare project to develop in the West End which was indigenous to the area and staffed by local youngsters.

The idea of a legal service for the West End community developed out of the Summer Programme. On 15 June

1970, Phil Cohen issued a 'provisional outline of legal scheme'. He claimed that 'the police in conjunction with Westminster City Council have decided to clear the West End and in particular Piccadilly of all the young people who normally make it their base during the summer'. He proposed a scheme to inform kids in the West End of their rights and to provide, in conjunction with the National Council for Civil Liberties, a support structure for those who were arrested. A panel of solicitors would be available, and a twenty-four-hour emergency service was to be established. Later in the year premises were acquired at 29 Frith Street, Soho, and 'The Muggins Trust' was set up to sponsor a series of accommodation, civil rights, education and research programmes. A house was acquired in the Elephant and Castle district which would form a commune for 'the nucleus of the drop out scene around the Dilly over the past two years'. The house would be an experiment in dropping back in a community situation. In November, Street Bond was announced as 'a legal advice centre designed to meet the needs of young people who are on the scene around the West End', and in December the name was changed to Street Aid. In June 1971, Street Aid moved to larger premises in 33 Southampton Street, Covent Garden.

The philosophical position of Street Aid is basically the same as that of the original 'Commune of the Streets' of 1968.

Unlike many agencies in the West End which simply endorse the 'official' solution, Street Aid believes that we have to create alternative structures to the whole 'children's zoo' set up of straight society and to work in and on the scene to improve it, to make it into a real alternative.

Although Street Aid has tended to distort and misrepresent the views of other agencies and to view them as hostile, their criticism of much conventional social work thinking seems to me to be correct. By their tremendous aggression and paranoia they have alienated many of the agencies to whom they turned regularly for help and advice. Yet I am sure the emergence of Street Aid was a very necessary stage in the development of the West End. For the first time the kids around Piccadilly began to take social action and to reject the paternalism of the social work machine.

Throughout the 144 Piccadilly affair, as at other times, the Press referred to the squatters as the 'hippies'. But the West End has never contained a genuine hippy culture which might be compared to that of San Francisco or other areas of psychedelic drug use. The London psychedelic drug culture has been geographically located for the most part in districts such as Notting Hill and Chelsea rather than in Soho. It has been in the streets of 'Scene W.11.' that much of the thinking of the Underground has taken place, and it is here that welfare bodies like Release and BIT have been established. Soho and its adjoining area has at various times provided specific locations for action in the movement: Better Books in Charing Cross Road where many of the gurus have met, UFO in Tottenham Court Road which for a while was the scene of wild psychedelic happenings, the Arts Lab in Drury Lane, and so on. But what is meant by 'hippy' and 'Underground'? The conventional media tend to use 'hippy' to describe anyone with long hair, or whose dress and philosophy deviate from the accepted standards. The term arose in the Haight-Ashbury where it was originally the name of a political group, Haight Independent Proprietors. It subsequently came to be used of those who aligned themselves with the new philosophy which came out of the Haight-Ashbury culture. It was here too, in

Haight-Street, that the Psychedelic Shop, the world's first 'head' store, opened in January 1966, and this was followed by the Trips Festival at Longshoreman's Hall. It was the first really big acid convention. The following year came the World's First Human Be-In in Golden Gate Park, San Francisco, with Timothy Leary, Allen Ginsberg and other notables in attendance. It was out of these events that the hippy culture grew.

The Underground in its origins goes back further, to about 1964 when the term first came into use in New York. It was used to describe films and magazines which were totally alien to the established media and which used sexual and religious weapons in the attack on the establishment. The Underground writers were concerned about Vietnam and Civil Rights, and they paid homage to protest singers like Joan Baez and Bob Dylan. Bookshops were opened and happenings took place in various cities. In Britain, the Underground could be seen as a minority growth out of the anti-bomb movement. In the Peace Café in Fulham Road and elsewhere, a culture grew up which looked towards the beat generation in the United States for its inspiration. Jeff Nuttall has outlined the historical background very well in his *Bomb Culture*. The matured British Underground as it appeared after 1967 was a fusion of this older political tradition and the newer ideas of the hippy movement.

The hippy philosophy of 1967 stressed the supreme importance of love, honesty and non-violence, and the value of psychedelic drugs for recreation as well as for spiritual enlightenment, and it rejected the values of capitalist society, the work ethic, and the civil and religious establishments. Unlike the revolutionary, the hippy did not oppose the establishment in a face-to-face conflict, but turned his back on it, preferring to build a new society within the crumbling ruins of the old. So arose the term 'alternative society', a term which in a few years has become a reality. It is important to emphasize that the hippy movement was essentially a moral protest: as Caroline Coon said in a talk at St Anne's in 1968, the hippy is 'the product of a society whose moral spirit is lower than it has been for some time'. To hippy culture, it is the mainstream western society which is materialistic, decadent, unspiritual, and lacking any moral standards or values.

The most significant visible sign of the growth of the Underground has been the spread of such papers and journals as *International Times, Oz, Rolling Stone,* and more recently, *Frendz* and *Ink.* Geoffrey Ashe, welcoming *International Times* in its issue of 23 August 1968, claimed that it represented 'the voice of a new kind of revolution . . . the beginning of a free creative countersociety, self-generated from the depths in a spirit of love, a clean break, a fresh start.' During the summer of 1969, a small booklet *Project Free London* began to circulate widely on the Underground scene. It gave information on how to obtain free accommodation, clothes, food, entertainment, travel and social services. I was the third item on page one, and was amused to find that the booklet printed not only my phone number but also the name and address of the Soho coffee bar where, it was claimed, I was most likely to be found! The booklet was later reprinted in Richard Neville's *Play Power.* It was the first serious attempt at a directory of facilities in the alternative society. Nicholas Saunders followed it with his *Alternative London* which has now become the standard reference book.

Within the hippy culture and among large sections of young people in our society, cannabis has become the new social drug. It is smoked primarily for pleasure, but its central position in social protest should not be ignored. Dr

David Smith, writing of the United States, has pointed out that 'in analysing the various youth protest movements —whether political activists and the Peace and Freedom party, centered in Berkley, or the Bohemians in Haight-Ashbury—one finds a number of common slogans: 'End the war in Vietnam, eliminate racism, and legalize marijuana'. In Britain, cannabis is used by many young people who stand outside the Underground and the hippy scene, but even here one can see how it symbolizes the gulf between the generations. In the early 1960s the drug was used by some of the young intellectuals in the peace movement, and *Peace News,* in its issue of 5 February 1965, had been one of the first papers to call for legalization. Soon after this cannabis began to spread among wider sections of youth, and it would be quite wrong today to associate cannabis use exclusively with any particular type of young person.

I doubt whether an objective assessment of cannabis use is possible until the next generation. In the meantime, the view of the Wootton Report of 1968 that long-term consumption of the drug in moderate doses has no harmful effects (paragraph 29) seems to me to sum up the world literature fairly well. It is not true, though it is often said, that there has been little research on the use of cannabis in its social setting. There is an enormous literature, and much of it is discussed in the studies by David Smith, E.R. Bloomquist, Erich Goode and John Kaplan in the United States, and by Michael Schofield and myself in this country. Certainly there is a great deal of research, pharmacological, sociological and medical, which needs to be done. But there is no justification for the exaggerated claims about 'escalation' and 'cannabis psychosis' which are often made, and the constant repetition of which causes young people to lose confidence in any information on drugs emanating from adult sources.

The pressure for a change in the law on cannabis has increased since the Soma Research Association placed a full-page advertisement in *The Times* on 24 July 1967, claiming that the law was 'immoral in principle and unworkable in practice'. I was critical of the advertisement at the time though I later joined the council of Soma. My general feeling at present is that the harm done by the law on cannabis far exceeds any harm which might result from the drug itself. The Soma advertisement did not argue, as many people have thought, for legalization of cannabis, and I doubt whether legalization is practicable as an immediate measure, but I think it will come in the next generation. It will raise some problems, but my feeling is that such a measure would do more good than harm.

The slogans 'Burn Pot, Not People' and 'Make Love, Not War' indicate that much of contemporary attitudes to drugs and sexuality is related to a rejection of militarism and the capitalist system. The Underground has, since 1967, become more explicitly political. The influence of Marcuse has been strong among the heads in the United States, and the language of liberation has brought together the Black Power movement, the politicized hippies and the student rebels. Violence has become more and more characteristic of the scene. What began as a subculture has now become a counter-culture.

The young people in Soho, however, have not been much affected by the new political mood. The majority of the drifters whom we met around Piccadilly would not be described as 'drop-outs' in the usual sense: they were more 'throw outs', failures of the system, social rejects. In youth work jargon, they were the 'young drifters'. In 1966 the Salvation Army workers at Regent Hall in Oxford Street felt the challenge of the young drifters, and opened an all-night club on Fridays called the Rink Club.

It attracted very large numbers of young people who were not part of the West End scene as well as regular numbers of young drifters and vagrants. It was as an attempt to help the young vagrants that the Rink Project grew out of the Rink Club, and subsequently, with the help of a grant from the Inner London Education Authority, it became one of three experimental youth projects operating in Soho. Originally the workers used the Rink Club as their base, but in 1968 they were lent the Undercroft of St Martin-in-the-Fields, which became known to thousands of young people all over the country as 'the crypt'. The crypt was open every day except Sunday between 9.00 a.m. and 5.00 p.m. and was staffed by youth workers of the Rink Project. In the early stages, Norman Croucher, a St Martin's worker, was in charge of the work, but later the Salvationists assumed responsibility, and the project, although it was on church premises, became virtually independent of St Martin's. Primarily the youngsters used the crypt for sleep, but advice and help was available if they wanted it, and the workers found that it provided the initial contact point within the vagrant community. From the crypt they moved out to coffee bars, tea stalls and clubs used by young vagrants. Under Alistair Cox, now the leader of the City Centre Project in Manchester, and Rod Moore, who left to join a course in youth and community work, the activity of the Rink expanded considerably, and during 1968-70 I enjoyed a very close relationship with its workers. We started to hold informal meetings each Monday night in St Anne's, when we could discuss individual problems, and, with help from a Jungian analyst, we established a series of group sessions to study difficulties of relationship, motivation and so on, amongst ourselves.

Throughout 1970, however, difficulties from two directions faced the Rink Project workers. The first came from the relationship with St Martin's Church, from whom the crypt was borrowed. The Rink workers felt that there was little real contact between what they were trying to do and the church upstairs. Relations in fact continued to deteriorate, and in 1970 the crypt was closed. Whatever the real reasons for the closure may have been, it was widely interpreted by young people in the area as a rejection of the Project by the Church authorities and by the establishment. The Church, it was claimed, had sponsored and tolerated a project while it was safe, but got cold feet and opted out as soon as it became risky. I do not think that this was an entirely fair criticism, but there is no doubt that in their philosophy and approach, the church and the Project were on quite different wavelengths. As it happened, the Rink workers very quickly found their feet in the field of detached work, and, while they found the lack of a base a disadvantage, they took the loss of the crypt as a sign for a change in direction. The Project moved out much more into the vagrant culture. They were probably glad and relieved to have lost their last formal link with the institutional Church.

The more serious and insuperable difficulty was ultimately a theological one. Some of the young Salvationists who ran the Rink Project had university backgrounds, while others were widely read in current sociology, youth work methods, and social casework, criminology, and so on. Theologically, their teachers were Harvey Cox, Van Buren, Tillich, and John Robinson. But their spiritual home was Regent Hall where worship and spirituality were expressed in the forms of nineteenth-century revivalism. There was a quite fantastic gulf between theology and spirituality among these young Salvationists. At Regent Hall it was Major Fred Brown, the commanding officer, one of the few Salvationists who attempted serious theological thought, who alone held

together the old and the young. But the future for Fred
Brown was bleak, and in 1970, after the publication of his
Secular Evangelism, he was dismissed from the Army.
Soon after Fred's dismissal, the Rink Project came to an
end, though it was rescued by, and absorbed into, the
Soho Project.

In many respects the history of what happened to the
Rink Project was tragic. It exposed the inability of the
Salvation Army to understand the social revolutions of
the twentieth century. There was an almost total compre-
hension gap, a genuine bewilderment and lack of awareness of what the young Rink workers were up to. The
Salvationist hierarchy were perplexed. On the one hand
they liked to exhibit the Rink Project as the living proof
of their concern for drug addicts, beatniks and drifters.
On the other hand, they were more and more concerned
that the theology and methods of Alistair and Rod and
their friends were totally alien to Salvationist thinking.
Here was a radical break with the proselytizing mentality,
the band meeting, and the street corner testimony. The
Rink Project made no attempt to evangelize. Only in
name was it connected with the Salvation Army. The
extent of the gulf can be seen in an article which the Rink
Project workers wrote in *Vanguard,* the Salvation Army
youth magazine in August 1969. Here they put forward
six principles for a 'mature relationship'.

(a) The two parties come together on equal terms. There
     is no stance of superiority/inferiority.
(b) There is no desire on the part of one to manipulate the
     other for his own end. We do not make our
     relationship conditional on a projected image of what
     we would like the other to become.
(c) It is slow to form and depends on consistency and
     persistency of presence.

(d) There is no place for haranguing, preaching or giving of advice.

(e) There is no concern for the classification we so often tend to impose on the individual. What does concern us is the degree of liberation that our relationships afford. There is consequently persistent concern for justice and a refusal to tolerate injustice.

(f) Our Christian concern is often best communicated through the trivial. We seek too often to talk about ultimates in a vacuum. These ultimates are best expressed through the sharing of a meal, the regular visit, the honest reaction, the warm pleasure of getting to know a person.

This represents an approach which is totally at variance with Salvation Army methods of evangelism. If the Army had contained in its ranks any serious theologians, or if it had been capable of taking seriously the challenge of Fred Brown's thought, then some change from within might have been conceivable. It was not to be so. But I believe, as a non-Salvationist who has had close contacts with the Army and learned much from it, that the death of the Rink Project was only a foretaste of further troubles within the Army, unless there are major changes soon.

From the beginning of our work with young people, the phenomenon of homelessness loomed very large. On 22 April 1968, I gave a talk to the Westminster Christian Council, an ecumenical group of Christians in the area, on accommodation needs for young people within the City. A Social Responsibility Working Party set up by the Council in 1967 had reported, not surprisingly, that the most pressing need in the City was for accommodation for the large and increasing numbers of homeless youth. On 3 April 1968, the Medical Officer of Health for the City of Westminster called a conference of all those concerned with the care of drug addicts in the City. One reason for calling the conference was a concern that 'unless a unified policy is agreed by all the parties concerned there may well be some overlapping of effort and perhaps over-provision of services and this, of course, should be avoided'. Nothing resulted from the conference although a number of people stressed the extreme urgency of the situation. In fact, we have found over the years that, in the field of accommodation for the homeless, the statutory bodies are often extremely unhelpful, and tend to leave most of the difficult problems to voluntary workers.

In November 1969 a group of us including the Rink Project workers and a number of members of the Simon Community house in Camden Town, became very conscious of a major gap in our West End work. All the agencies in Soho appeared to be spending most of their time in helping the same individuals, the 'West End regulars' who were known to us all. But at the same time, thousands of new youngsters were pouring into and through the West End, more new kids were getting involved with prostitution, new faces were appearing on the drug scene, and very little preventive work was being attempted. We felt that a new emphasis was needed in trying to avert the casualties and crises whose consequences we saw daily. As we discussed this, we realized that beneath us the basement of St Anne's stood derelict, unused for years, a virtual rubbish dump. So the idea of 'Centrepoint' was born.

We called our new project 'Centrepoint' because it was geographically at the centre point of Soho, and also as an ironic contrast to the other Centrepoint, the luxury office block which stood empty and useless a few hundred yards away. On 16 December we opened the converted basement as an overnight crisis centre where young people who were new to the West End could be accommodated and given immediate advice and help. The people we had in mind were new arrivals, youngsters who had come to London in search of work, or who had run away from difficult home situations and who were at risk of becoming homeless and destitute. We worked out a system of staffing with the Simon Community, a body which for six years had been involved with homeless, isolated people, and it was through Simon helpers that the project got off the ground. Neil McGhee, a little Scotsman, and Bill Rice from Limerick, were our first project leaders, and did a fantastic job. In the first two months we took in 600 youngsters, and the figure had risen to 1,000 by the end of three months. Of these, 670 were newcomers, of whom eighty-nine were from Glasgow, forty-five from Manchester, and thirty-five from Dublin. Fifteen per cent of the newcomers were Scottish.

In the first year of its existence, Centrepoint was taking in an average of twenty people each night, about 5,000 over the whole year. Our clients came from three main sources: Euston Station; voluntary agencies such as BIT, Samaritans or St Martin-in-the-Fields; and the local 'grapevine'. The contact with Euston Station proved immensely useful, for here the newcomers from the north arrived. Our workers found the British Transport police enthusiastic and helpful, and we soon established a practice of having a Centrepoint car at Euston each morning about 1.00 a.m. Other organizations were a main source of referral. In particular 'Benburb Base' a centre for the care of Irish youth, was tremendously cooperative. They provided us on three nights each week with several sisters, a priest, and other workers, and we referred new Irish youngsters to them for extensive counselling, accommodation or employment. During 1970, as a result of the troubles in Northern Ireland, we found an increasing number of Belfast youngsters arriving. But it was Glasgow and Scotland generally which provided the largest single minority group, and it is important that a Scottish equivalent to Benburb Base should be established in London as soon as possible.

In November 1970 Centrepoint and the Simon Community separated. The split was inevitable because the supervision and control of the project was becoming more and more chaotic. The Simon Community depends largely on volunteers who may be very immature, inexperienced or extremely disturbed and unbalanced individuals. Some of the Simon workers were excellent and responsible, and without their help Centrepoint would not have become established at all. But the situation was so bad at the end of 1970 that we found it necessary to assume complete control and set up Centrepoint as an independent project. A new committee was set up with Harry Knight, an estate agent and a deeply committed Christian, as chairman. In 1971 he was succeeded by Ben Harrison, the secretary of the Church of England Council for Social Aid, who for years had been a source of support for our work. We were fortunate in obtaining a number of large donations from individuals, and later were given several sizeable grants, including one from the Supplementary Benefits Commission, and so were able to employ a full-time director, David Nairn, in February 1970. David Nairn had previously been in charge of a rehabilitation unit for alcoholics, and was closely involved with research activity. He provided exactly the right help we needed at the consolidation stage of Centrepoint: a strong, experienced worker, with a deep knowledge of human problems and a wide range of contacts. Our hope for Centrepoint is that it will expand into a twenty-four hour service, providing extensive referral and counselling where necessary, but its primary role remains that of an emergency all-night service for newcomers.

The Simon Community had been active in the field of homelessness long before the establishment of Centrepoint. Its original work was with methylated spirit drinkers in Stepney, and the first Simonlight hostel was in fact at 84 Cable Street, the building in which I had lived when it was a Franciscan mission. The next Simonlight was in Sclater Street, Bethnal Green, where there was a fierce clash with the local authority. The main London work was established at Malden Road, Camden Town, where at different times young drug addicts, homeless families and new arrivals were accommodated. But a series of difficulties led to a schism between the London Simon Community and the communities in the provinces. As a result, the various Simon houses outside London banded together into the Cyrenians, while the London and Liverpool houses with the farm in Kent remained as the Simon Community Trust. The Trust, through a series of pamphlets and prolific Press activity, has continued to draw public attention to the problems of homelessness and vagrancy. It is a pity that their zeal has not always been accompanied by strict factual accuracy, and that irresponsible organization has often led their projects into chaotic muddles which can do positive harm.

Nevertheless, while these serious criticisms must stand, all who work in the homeless field owe a tremendous debt to the Simon Community. I think that they have been leaders in two directions in particular. First, in helping to eliminate the 'we-they' syndrome in social work, and to emphasize the unity of helpers and helped. Secondly, in rejecting the dividing and labelling of human beings into 'problem' categories—alcoholics, psychopaths, drug addicts, and so on—and treating them as human beings with a wide range of needs and difficulties. The early Simon houses refused to categorize people and did not attempt to be an amateur social work department. Their houses of hospitality were pointers towards what the Christian Church as a whole ought to be: a non-judgmental, caring, loving community, accepting people as they are in Christ's name. It is worth remembering that Simon, although it has accepted workers of all faiths and none, has persistently maintained that its ideals and inspiration are Christian, and Anton Wallich-Clifford, its founder, at least, seems to view it as a new-style religious order. In Ireland, where Simon houses are more closely allied with the Roman Catholic Church, this vision may be realized earlier than in England.

Another body with which we have worked in the field of homelessness is Christian Action. David Brandon, who has acted as a social work consultant to both Christian Action and Centrepoint, was a friend of mine from Hoxton days, when he ran the London County Council's Welfare Office for the Homeless at Charing Cross. His publications *The Treadmill* (1970) and *Homeless in London* (1971) have been major contributions to the fight for better housing and care of homeless people. With David's help, Centrepoint was involved in 1971 in a protest to the Registrar-General about the Population Census. We pointed out that while protests were being made, rightly in my view, about the questions on birthplaces of parents, there were a large number of homeless people who would not have a chance of answering the questions at all! A few weeks after the official Census, Christian Action conducted its own Census of the Homeless, using Centrepoint as its headquarters. In November 1971, Christian Action itself moved into Soho, and opened a shelter for homeless women in Greek Street, very near to St Anne's House.

One of the most disturbing trends which we have seen at Centrepoint is the rapid movement of some youngsters from home to situations of extreme danger. Many of those who came through Centrepoint during 1970 and 1971 were under twenty, few had used Government reception centres, and most had left home during the previous week or month. Provision for young homeless people in London is appallingly inadequate. Apart from Centrepoint and a few other places, all the beds in hostels, lodging houses and shelters are strictly segregated. Often they are all full. Over and over again, we found ourselves in positions of complete helplessness.

But although the numbers of new arrivals were increasing and more young people were coming into the world of the temporarily homeless, the West End drug culture was very much in decline during 1970 and 1971. This was true at a number of levels. After the setting up of the treatment centres, the majority of heroin addicts left Piccadilly, and only used it for surplus supplies if they ran short. The old 'junkies' corner' was reduced to a small hard core of semi-vagrant addicts, and the aura of Eros as a junkie mecca gradually faded. The changed method of dealing with prescriptions was a crucial factor in the decline of the West End, for after 1968 the clinics posted addicts' prescriptions to the chemist nearest to their home. As a result, Boots' at Piccadilly Circus ceased to play a central role for cashing prescriptions, and tended to be used more by the vagrant or semi-vagrant addicts. In addition to this, not only did a number of the established 'Piccadilly junkies' die from overdoses in 1969-70, but the graph for increases in heroin addiction nationaly had, at last, begun to fall. Dr Ian James, formerly Medical Officer at Brixton Prison, in a paper given at the International Conference on Addiction at Cardiff in 1970, showed with abundant statistical material, that the heroin epidemic was probably over.Certainly in Soho we were seeing few new addicts after 1970: we only saw the old addicts who kept coming back.

Meanwhile, Soho had begun to decline as a club quarter among young people. Of course the big music clubs for jazz, folk, rhythm and blues, and rock, remained at a fairly static level. But the subcultural life of the club-going youth was declining. Laurie Little, an experienced youth worker, described the beginnings of this decline in an article in the Soho Project Report in 1969.

> Since 1963-4, the time of The Discotheque in Wardour Street and the rash of clubs run by Nash; the time of pep-pill parties in the Leicester Square conveniences— when for a moment innocent girls and boys felt they had latched on to something really *new*—the word has come back—the West End's had it. Certainly the action in the last two or three years has been much more on the perimeter of London: a whole club-going sector of the youth of Inner London turned their backs on the pathetic con of Soho and the West End, and it's doubtful if they will ever need to come back.

Certainly by 1967, it was the more 'deviant' kids who used the clubs, and by 1970, even these seemed less in evidence. Most of the young people whom I knew in the gay clubs and other all-night centres in 1967-68 have now left the West End. So gradually Soho has become more the refuge for the severely disturbed, fringe psychopathic youth, whose degree of alienation is very great. The gay clubs have tended to move further west towards Earl's Court, Kensington and Chelsea. Lyceums and large dance halls have sprung up in the suburbs. The entertainment role of the inner West End has declined. At the same time, the drug scene has shifted its focal points. The West End drug culture has passed its peak and is now on the wane: other parts of the country are now at, or will soon reach, the stage that Soho was at a number of years ago.

What of the pill-taking youth? Viewed solely from a pharmacological perspective, Soho has always been primarily a pill scene. It is the amphetamines which have dominated the drug market: not illicitly manufactured materials as in the United States, but tablets and capsules which have emanated from well-known pharmaceutical houses. This perhaps needs to be stressed as it is sometimes claimed by ill-informed persons that illicit manufacture plays a major role here. Thus the *Guardian* on 9 July 1971 reported: 'Schoolboys are helping to make amphetamines in laboratories which supply a quarter of the drugs black market, a police surgeon told a conference of the British Medical Association in London yesterday.' This is complete nonsense. The overwhelming majority of amphetamines which circulate among drug abusers are licitly manufactured, and reach the black market by a variety of routes: over-prescribing and thefts from warehouses, manufacturers, and retail chemists are the major ones. It is these substances which have provided the bulk of the drugs which are used illegally in the streets of Soho.

What value are the amphetamines? At one time they were used in a variety of conditions: fatigue, depression, overweight, and so on. Their use as a 'wakeamine' made them popular during the Second World War when, in the form of Benzedrine, they were issued in enormous quantities to the armed forces. The earliest groups of abusers of 'purple hearts' (Drinamyl) in the 1950s consisted in fact, of middle-aged women who used them as slimming agents. The psychiatric use of amphetamines became virtually obsolete with the appearance of tranquillizers and anti-depressants. They were found to be virtually useless as slimmers. The Ministry of Health's Annual Report of 1955, which described them as 'relatively non-toxic', claimed that addiction to them was rare and that few risks accompanied their use. Three years later Dr Philip Connell published his *Amphetamine Psychosis!* But the danger of the amphetamines had been described long before this in the Japanese and American literature. In 1968 a Working Party of the British Medical Association reported that there were no real indications for their use except in the treatment of narcolepsy, a very rare condition.

Yet these obsolete drugs continue to be manufactured. In Ipswich and several other areas, doctors and chemists have co-operated in implementing a voluntary ban on amphetamines, and it has been suggested that this should be attempted nationally. It would be silly to see this as panacea for all drug ills. Drug abuse will not be eliminated by more and more controls on availability. Nevertheless, the present situation, where therapeutically useless substances are poured forth onto the market, is indefensible. It is little use to have a few overworked individuals in Soho and elsewhere attempting to rescue casualties from a swamp if no attention is paid to the more important problem of draining the swamp.

In my book *A Practical Guide to the Drug Scene* I suggested that there were five qualities which were particularly necessary in the priest who ministers among alienated young people, and they bear repetition here. None of them are qualities which I feel I possess adequately, and indeed I tend to view much of my failure as a pastor as the result of a failure to cultivate them. First, naturalness. There is an old catholic maxim that grace perfects nature and does not destroy it: the Spirit of God works through human personalities with all their peculiarities, inhibitions, eccentricities and weaknesses. I find it very sad to see priests attempting to assume a role in order to gain effect, an assumed 'with-it-ness'. Certainly there is a desperate need for more beat priests, more hippy priests, more gay priests, more revolutionary priests, and one of our major problems in the Church is that so often we draw our ordinands from a fairly monochrome section of the population. The reason why ordinands are often out of touch with the growing youth culture is that they come from sections of the community which are least representative of the community as a whole—though this pattern is changing. But the answer is not for ordinands or priests to assume a facade, a way-out cover-up for a straight, conventional individual. We must never pretend to be what we are not for the sake of our image, for the sake of 'relevance', or for any other reason.

Secondly, a non-condescending approach. There is still too much paternalism around, the soup-kitchen approach, which treats people as objects of our pity: they are there to be done good to. We need to grow in humility and to care about people for their own sakes. 'If there's one thing I hate', said one young man, 'it's being worked amongst.'

Thirdly, the absence of the 'parsonic voice' and image. I really believe that the 'parsonic voice' has done a tremendous amount of damage. It is not just the dull monotony and the false impression of insincerity which it gives. It is more the cultivated style of talking *at* people, not *to* them. It is a corrupting thing which spreads like a virus: you can watch young men acquiring the voice, the intonation, the silly mannerisms, the precious, affected air. With the voice and mannerisms goes the image of the nice, refined clergyman, very fragile and easily shocked, insulated from the real world of conflict and suffering, protected by his collar and dark suit from real human contact. So many youngsters feel that the priest is not really human, and that to talk about sex, for instance, would shock and shake him. Too often I am afraid they are right. Certainly the natural, spontaneous way in which many young people talk about their sex hang-ups as well as their sexual pleasure would embarrass and shock a good number of inhibited clergymen. So the discussion takes place when he is not there, either because the people are too kind to offend him, or too scared to approach him. So it is that the priest often misses out on the central areas of human life.

One result of this, sadly, is that clergy conversations tend to become pathetically trivial. One can see this at two levels. Because many people find clergy difficult, if not impossible, to talk to in a relaxed way, they restrict their conversations to superficialities. But also the clergy themselves, through an excessive cultivation of clerical gatherings, tend to talk about ecclesiastical affairs as if the whole world depended on them. The late Canon Stanley Evans once commented of one clergyman: 'Only sur-rounded by clergymen can he be happy: the superficial *bonhomie* of the common-room or the gossip of the sacristy appears to be necessary to his salvation.' I think that an excess of clergy meetings is as bad for the soul as an excess of alcohol is for the body. They encourage so much of the clerical image which alienates us from ordinary people.

Fourthly, a sense of humour. One of the authentic signs of freedom is laughter. I think that it is very important for priests to be laughed at. In fact, my wife sees one of the main functions of the priest's wife to be 'taking the mickey' out of her husband, so that people can see through the clerical image. A ridiculously well-developed sense of the irrational and absurd is really important in contemporary youth culture. If all the clergy started to take *Private Eye* instead of some of the dreadful church papers, it would be a help.

Finally, confidentiality and trustworthiness. The priest needs to be seen as a reliable person whose confidence can be taken for granted. The issue of confidentiality is of the greatest importance. One's whole reputation as a priest may be damaged by a breakdown at this point. If one is not trusted, one cannot hope to be heard.

But, in the end, any recital of qualities and virtues must sound artificial and unreal. One cannot learn to be a true pastor from any book. I cannot hope to convey more than a glimmering of how one approaches pastoral work simply by writing about it: so much depends on the kind of person we become. We can only show the fruits of the Spirit if we are filled with the Spirit.

5

A NEW SPIRITUALITY?

For many people any connection between drug use and the spiritual quest would seem far-fetched, and the very suggestion of such a connection would seem quite monstrous. A good deal of Christian ministry in the field of drug abuse has started from the assumption that the drug scene is an evil from which young people must be rescued. Soho too has been seen as a centre of evil, and has attracted evangelical crusaders as a light attracts moths. So Billy Graham paid a ritual visit to Old Compton Street in 1965. So Piccadilly Circus is regularly visited by zealous Christians who hand out tracts and offer free food and sometimes gospel music. At times one gets the feeling that Piccadilly consists solely of evangelical Christians, social workers and tourists, each group thinking that the other groups are the local indigenous population. Very often during my time in Soho we have discovered some new evangelistic campaign which has sprung up without any consultation with, or approach to, the Christians on the spot. These activities seem to show little or no understanding of the common order of the Body of Christ in which 'bonded and knit together by every constituent joint, the whole frame grows through the due activity of each part, and builds itself up in love.' (Ephesians 4.16).

Once a group of students from a Bible college descended upon Soho and posted stickers saying 'Faith Not Filth' on all the strip clubs. They then returned to their homes in other districts, leaving the local Christian community in Soho to apologize for them and clear up the mess, and to try and undo the harm which they had done. It has probably not occurred to such sincere people that the pastoral work of the Body of Christ in Soho might be set back a few years by this kind of activity, or even that there are Chritians living and working there, whose ministry might be affected by these escapades. I regard many of these crusaders as a positive menace. They are incredibly silly, obsessed with sex, have a distorted view of evil, and see Soho as the 'sin centre' of London. They are aggressive., intolerant, and insensitive, rushing clumsily into situations which they do not understand and dabbling with problems which they have not studied. This does not apply to all evangelicals, but it does apply to many of the people who seem to be drawn to Soho. In addition, some of these groups seem to contain a number of highly unbalanced individuals who are drawn to work here through their own psychological disturbances more than for the good of the district. Many young people have been put off Christianity as a result of their contact of and experiences with these groups.

The aggressive naivety which is characteristic of much evangelical work in the field is exhibited in their literature. Factual inaccuracy seems to be a fundamental prerequisite in the writers. The best known evangelical writings are those of the American Pentecostalist, David Wilkerson, author of *The Cross and the Switchblade* (1962) and numerous other books. These books show a burning faith in God and a commitment to Christ and the salvation of souls. They also show a degree of intolerance, disrespect for facts, and an unbalanced approach which is very disturbing and frightening. Thus *The Cross and the Switchblade* tells us that 'marijuana . . . quickly leads to the use of heroin', a view contrary to all the evidence. In an article in *The Pentecostal Evangel* in

1968, David Wilkerson said, 'I consider marijuana the most dangerous drug used today.' and claimed that 'marijuana users become just as 'hooked' as persons addicted to heroin.' Teenagers are advised to 'report it to the police immediately' if they see another teenager smoking marijuana. The view, accepted by most scholars that 'the dangers of marijuana have been overrated' is dismissed by David Wilkerson as 'an outright lie'.

This combination of intolerance and sheer ignorance cannot be excused by reference to the writer's practical experience. Proximity to a situation is no guarantee of reliability or objective analysis. Indeed it is sad that many of those who work closely with drug abusers are among the most inaccurate and unreliable commentators. David Wilkerson's writing is full of misleading comments. Thus his book *Purple Violet Squish* (1969) tells us that 'a hippy is one who removes himself from physical and intellectual reality' and 'believes only in himself'. The hippy scene is dismissed as a 'bogus gospel ... as old as the devil himself.' We are told that 'the LSD movement is headed down into the same dark cave where all the radical new theologians are hiding'. Father Philip Berrigan's action of pouring blood on draft files is described as a 'bizarre action of the unique yippie movement'. Wilkerson has no time for 'misguided liberals' or leftist priests, or for the Underground Press which supports them. But neither does he care for 'hippy evangelists'. 'Take off your love beards and grow up', he tells them. He warns that 'the church is not a cheap crash pad for hippies'. The magazines which come from Teen Challenge show the same degree of arrogance and insensitivity.

I find this kind of evangelical writing terribly sad, because the love of Christ does not surely show itself in contempt for the views of others. Our zeal for truth and refusal to compromise with evil ought never to lead us to a disrespect for accurate scholarship or to an inability to listen and to learn from those with whom we disagree. Fortunately, not all evangelical Christians working in the drug scene are of this type. I think particularly of the wonderful ministries of Barbara and Doug Henry at the Coke Hole Trust near Andover, or of Frank Wilson at Life for the World in Gloucestershire. I am proud to number these Christian workers among my friends. They show a deep faith and humility which puts me to shame, and serves as a source of inspiration and example. We have had particularly close links with the Coke Hole, where numerous young people from Soho have received help and been brought to life in Christ. My criticisms of some evangelical attitudes must not be taken as an attack on all evangelicals. But I have felt so deeply how much harm has been done to the Christian cause by the impact of the type of attitude and literature which I have described.

One of the presuppositions of many Christian commentators is that the drug culture is one facet of a wholesale attack upon Christian moral standards. This is a viewpoint which would presumably be shared by such movements as the Festival of Light which talks of 'moral pollution'. David Wilkerson certainly sees the hippy scene as being characterized by sin, emptiness and futility. Against the decadence of the runaway generation, he places the world of the squares. 'Squares do not demonstrate nor do they question every cultural, ethical, political and religious value of the day. Squares are conventional and conforming. They don't burn their draft cards, and even wear service uniforms with pride. Squares are wheels who make the world go 'round'. Before we go any further, let me confess that I'm a square.' So Christianity becomes identified with the square world, with conformism and with the established order.

I do not accept this position. Rather I view much of

current drug abuse as one aspect of a protest against the decadence and materialism of our western society. To the hippy it is the establishment which is immoral, and his attack upon it is primarily a spiritual one. I agree with Caroline Coon's view that the hippy represents a moral protest against 'a society whose moral spirit is lower than it has been for a long time'. But I would go further than this and say that the fundamental motivation behind the drug culture is a search for spirituality. The recent Interim Report of the Canadian Government Commission of Inquiry *The Non-Medical Use of Drugs* (1971) observed:

> We have been profoundly impressed by the natural and unaffected manner in which drug users have responded to the question of religious significance. They are not embarrassed by the mention of God. Indeed, as Paul Goodman has observed, their reactions are in interesting contrast to those of the 'God is dead' theologians. It may be an exaggeration to say that we are witnessing the manifestations of a genuine religious revival, but there does appear to be a definite revival of interest in the religious or spiritual attitude towards life.

With this comment a large section of the Underground would agree. So *Alternative London* observes: 'Over the past two centuries the established Christian churches have adapted themselves to please the scientists and intellectuals to a point where they have lost the essence of religion. Many young people are now disillusioned by the direction in which society is developing, and have become aware (often through drugs) that intellectualism cannot provide answers to the only important questions in life.'

The name of Timothy Leary is now inseparable from the psychedelic movement. It was Leary, dismissed from a position at Harvard in 1963, who firmly placed the LSD cult in a religious framework. 'It's the same old pursuit', said Leary. 'The aims of our religion are those of every religion in the past: we work to find the God within, the divinity which lies within each person's body.' Many of Leary's critics have misrepresented his position, and have given the impression that his view is that psychedelic drugs can of themselves produce instant mysticism. What he actually says, in *The Psychedelic Experience* and elsewhere, is that drugs can *help* to produce the religious experience. The right preparation and the 'right set and setting' were necessary. At the same time, it should be emphasized that Leary *does* state that the 'drug induced ecstasis is now called the psychedelic experience,' and claims that 'experiences of enlarged consciousness . . . have become available to anyone through the ingestion of psychedelic drugs'. This claim is the basis of the psychedelic religion.

It is a major claim but not a new one. William James in 1902 made the same claim about nitrous oxide, as did Benjamin Blood in 1874, and many devotees in earlier centuries about other drugs. The use of chemicals to induce religious experiences is a long-established phenomenon. I do not see any *a priori* reason to doubt the truth of the chemical claim. Experiences of enlarged consciousness, what Alan Watts calls 'cosmic consciousness', always involve alterations in body chemistry, and whether these chemical changes occur 'naturally' or are induced by the introduction of external chemicals, does not seem to me to alter the nature of the experience. The human body itself is a complex of biochemical forces. Moreover, the research on psychedelic drugs seems to support the view that the two kinds of experience are similar and at times identical. There is a good deal of data on this question in Masters and Houston's *The Varieties of Psychedelic Experience*. In 1970, I took part in a series of three programmes on BBC-2 TV entitled 'The Timeless Moment', in which the experiences under LSD, psychosis, and mystical religion were compared. The most detailed work has been done in the United States by Dr Walter Pahnke.

What I would strongly dispute is the relevance and value of the psychedelic experiences. The experiences of the mystics were evaluated and understood only in the context of a developing spiritual life. Any concern with the accumulation of experiences was condemned, as by St John of the Cross, for example, as a positive impediment to spiritual growth. In the drug culture, however, one sees precisely this obsession with 'experiences' for their own sake. There is a good deal of evidence that LSD can produce religious *experiences:* there is no evidence that it can produce religious *lives.* But Leary would dissent from this, and would claim that in fact the use of psychedelics has brought about a fundamental spititual change.

> They bring you into levels of reality which aren't structured because your mind can't structure them. But the panorama and the levels that you get into with LSD are exactly those areas which men have called the confrontation of God. The LSD trip is the classic visionary-mystic voyage . . . In the last six or seven years a small group of us, which has grown with almost miraculous rapidity, has brought about a change in the consciousness of the United States.

Whether or not Leary is right, there is no doubt that real changes in consciousness are occurring. In 1968, Dr Allan Cohen, a former research colleague of Leary's at Harvard, visited us at St Anne's. The *Guardian* on 14 September announced, 'Psychedelic drugs scene in search of spiritual guidance'. Allan and I became good friends , and in 1969 he returned, and addressed a crowded audience on 'LSD and the search for God'. In this he referred to his disillusionment with the psychedelic claims. Cohen sees the search for love and meaning as the real motivation of the psychedelic revolution, but he rejects the drug route to consciousness expansion. 'When you see the psychedelic leaders of the world after a gorgeously mystical brotherhood love session, as they are coming down, having a bitter argument about who should wash the dishes, a sense passes through one that somehow sainthood has been missed.' The psychedelic culture, Cohen claimed, had failed to show positive fruits in terms of spirituality. He points to the decay of Haight-Ashbury and suggests that heightened consciousness does not in fact result from chemical-induced experiences. Cohen and Leary agree that there has been a 'consciousness revolution', but Cohen sees the drug route as a diversion, an illusory path. So he argues for 'turning on' by an internal method, and he talks of 'a spiritual revolution which may dwarf in its impact any threatened economic or social-political revolution'.

In Berkeley, California, where Allan Cohen lives, the Committee for Psychedelic Drug Information publicizes his position. I met the leaders of the Committee in January 1970 in Berkeley and have maintained contact with them since then. This has been a valuable contact with the spiritual developments there. The inspiration for them, and for other ex-drug users, has been the Indian mystic Meher Baba, whose works on consciousness are among the best-known authoritative studies. It was the publication, by a young Sufi group in San Francisco, of a collection of Baba's utterances on LSD in a pamphlet entitled *God in a Pill?* which began a major change in the direction of many spiritual seekers on the West Coast. Cohen has described how a young friend and LSD enthusiast visited Nepal in 1965 and consulted Baba about psychedelic drugs, and has described the journey as 'a pilgrimage which became a focal point for the downfall of the psychedelic phantasy'. Basically, Baba's position and that of his followers (including Pete Townshend of 'The Who' who announced his rejection of drugs in 1969) is that the psychedelic experience is 'as far removed from reality as a mirage from water.' Reality is beyond them. So the Baba-lovers turn from the illusion to the reality.

We began to notice the movement away from chemical towards non-chemical approaches to spirituality in 1968. As well as the Baba movement, there was the growth in Chelsea of a community called 'Gandalf's Garden'. Gandalf is the White Wizard from Tolkien's *Lord of the Rings,* a major source book for the Underground mystical revival. Gandalf's role is to remain in Middle Earth and to liberate it from the dark powers. He is seen therefore as 'the mythological hero of the age'. The central figure in Gandalf's Garden was Muz Murray. Muz had a natural mystical experience in Cyprus which changed his whole approach to life and religion, and made him aware of the spiritual world. He returned to London in 1967 at the peak of the LSD epidemic, and became interested in the drug route. But he found LSD not only dangerous but also a purely 'horizontal' experience: that is, it could bring into consciousness experiences from the past and present, but could not take the subject into the future, as a natural mystical experience could. Numbers of those who were disillusioned with LSD turned towards mysticism of the Gandalf's Garden type as an alternative.

For a while a 'mystical scene magazine' entitled *Gandalf's Garden* was published, but in 1970 it was decided that the first priority was the establishment of ashrams, spiritual centres, throughout the country, and so the magazine ceased publication. *Gandalf's Garden* carried advertisements for a wide range of groups and facilities—meditation societies, vegetarian restaurants, mystical shops, and so on. It carried articles with titles like 'The Cosmic Continent', 'The Aetherius Society', 'The Sacred Zodiac of Glastonbury' and 'The Key to Self-Realization.' Contributors were not favourable to organized Christianity, which they saw as unspiritual and unrelated to the teaching of Jesus. One writer, commenting on the Billy Graham crusade, observed that 'an evening spent with Dr Graham is as spiritually rewarding as Mrs Dale's Diary,' and that the message was 'as bright and flashy and devoid of content as an empty Kellog's packet'. But they were not wholly unsympathetic to Christian ideas. Thus a Dominican friar wrote in one issue: 'When the apostles made their first public appearances they were so high that the people thought they must be drunk. And our whole thing began when an angel came to Mary and said, 'Rejoice!' We have no use at all for grey revolutionaries. We want people who really groove on our thing, people who find we turn them on . . . You can't have a utopia, at least not our sort of utopia, unless it turns people on.'

Another element in the recent spiritual revival has been the traditions surrounding Glastonbury and its Zodiac. Some young people claim that at the Chalice Well they discovered the influence of Jesus by direct experience. But they see Jesus as a great teacher or Avatar, born and reborn from age to age under many names. Glastonbury in seen by many young hippy seekers as a key to the future, and they have considerable sympathy with the off-beat type of Christianity which they associate with the Glastonbury myths. As Geoffrey Ashe, the authority on the Arthurian legends, wrote, 'Britain will begin to be reborn when Glastonbury is. The Giant Albion will begin to wake when his sons and daughters gather inside that enchanted boundary, and summon him with the right words, the right actions, a different life.'*

In Soho, particularly in Oxford Street and Piccadilly, the Hare Krishna chanters are well known figures. Their Temple is in Bloomsbury and from here they spend a large part of each day chanting the Hare Krishna mantra. According to their leader, A.C. Bhaktivedanta Swami, 'the transcendental vibration established by the chanting of the Hare Krishna mantra is a sublime method for reviving our transcendental consciousness'. It was in 1965 that A.C. Bhaktivedanta Swami, the founder of the International Society for Krishna Consciousness, arrived in the United States, and in October 1968, a small group of chanters arrived in London from San Francisco. Within a short while they had set up a commune and temple and made a record with the Beatles. They see the Hare Krishna mantra as the way both of awakening God-consciousness in everyone, and also of overcoming the distractions of the present Dark Age (Kali Yuga). The mantra is seen as a purifying process which cleanses the mind and the senses. Chanting in the street is important. 'The movement's work is done,' says one of their leaflets, 'by preaching and bringing the ecstatic sound vibrations to our brethren in the streets of all the major cities of the world . . . Krishna Consciousness is a movement that will bring universal peace and Divine Love to every being on this planet.' In London, the residents at the Temple follow a life of 'spiritual communion' based on the Hindu teachings on spiritual progress towards God-realization. There is no emphasis here on 'meditation' or on exploring the inner world, but rather on mental chanting and the chanting aloud of the Great Mantra.

* For further light on the Glastonbury Zodiac ideas see John Michell's books *The Flying Saucer Vision, A View Over Atlantis* and *City of Revelation.*

Among other sections of young people, however, meditation has been popular, ever since the Beatles became involved with Maharishi Mahesh Yogi in 1967. Here again, there is a sense of reaction against a Christianity which seems unconcerned with spirituality and which is seen as superficial. A good example of the general attitude towards the Church is contained in an interview with George Harrison in *International Times* on 29 August 1969. 'Now I don't want to put down the Christians, but it was only through India and through Hinduism and through yogis and through meditation that I learned about Christ and what Christ really meant and what he stood for, and what he still stands for and what he still is, because the Christ-consciousness is like the Krishna-consciousness which is absolute and is in every speck of creation. But this is why I never became a practising Christian, because like most people they go to church, and it's all that thing about, you know, Tommy Jones has got a brown suit on, and here comes Mrs Smith with her new hat. So in church there's no good vibes to pick up. It's a bore.' He went on to suggest that the Church was not much concerned with spiritual experience or with meditation. This is a common criticism made by many young people, and it is a just one.

All over the London scene therefore we were seeing a resurgence of spiritual concern. *Alternative London,* devoted twenty-one pages to mystical groups. It included very diverse groups: Hindu-orientated groups like the Divine Light Mission, the Rama Krishna Vedanta Centre and Kundalini Yoga centres, Buddhist and Sufi groups, and a large number of occult and spiritualistic sects. Astrology and flying saucers have caught on in some quarters, as has witchcraft. There is a spiritual revival of which, for the most part, the institutional Church seems totally unaware.

In 1970 I was anxious to see what form the post-LSD spiritual scene had taken in the United States. My impression is that there have been three particular directions in which people have tended to move. The first is the marked movement among many former LSD users towards magic, occultism, and mystical or quasi-mystical forms of religion. In a study of communes in North California, it was found that, while LSD and marijuana were still used in many cases, the total consumption of psycho-active chemicals was substantially less than the average American norm. The older hippies were turning to the communes, to non-chemical 'turn-ons' and to the eastern spiritual tradition.

One person who has studied the post-LSD scene in San Francisco very closely is Dr David Smith, the Medical Director of the Haight-Ashbury Free Clinic and Assistant Clinical Professor of Toxicology at the University of California Medical Centre. He claims that LSD in a psychedelic environment is producing real alterations in consciousness. He notes particularly that in working with chronic LSD users, 'one is continually impressed by their belief in magic and their intense study of metaphysical subjects'. Astrology is a major force in the lives of many young people in Haight-Ashbury, and it is not uncommon for an individual to alter a whole week's activities because of the behaviour of a passing meteorite. In a study of communes, David Smith pointed out that parents there often gave their children names derived from 'astrology, Eastern metaphysics, and psychedelic mysticism'. Some of the children's names were Oran, Morning Star, Rama Krishna, Ongo Ishi, Star, and Ora Infinitya. Thus, after entry into the psychedelic subculture, many straight, conventional young Americans have developed a magical frame of reference.

The second significant spiritual development in the

United States has been a growth of underground, radical Christian groups. The Berkeley Free Church, which I visited in 1970, is one of the best known 'liberated churches', and grew out of Dick York's street pastorate in the Telegraph Avenue district of Berkeley. 'Turn on to the liberated zone! The Free Church loves you', announced the sign in the entrance. The Church began by operating a twenty-four-hour switchboard and organizing 'crash pads', coping with bad trips, and providing psychological and spiritual help and counselling. It has been described as 'an ecumenical youth church with one foot in and one foot out of the establishment'. Its memorial service for Ho Chi Minh caused violent criticism from other local churches. The Free Church sees itself as part of a wider movement called the 'liberated church' which reaches across the United States. A directory *Win With Love* lists such free Christian communities around the country. Their basic theological approach is well expressed in John Pairman Brown's *The Liberated Zone,* and their liturgical ideas in *The Covenant of Peace.*

Out of the early street crisis ministry in Berkeley came two realizations. Dick York has expressed it in this way. 'First, that a paternalistic service ministry was not enough—that the only effective ministry for the Telegraph Avenue population was the development of a community, a youth church . . . (2) You cannot minister to alienated runaways, drug users and street people without addressing yourself to the causes of that alienation.' So the Free Church began to celebrate the 'Freedom Meal' and to pass its members through the waters of Baptism. The other local churches cried, 'That is not what we intended you to do at all!' 'We were a creation, it now seems', Dick York claims, 'to salve the conscience of the Berkeley Church establishment. So they could say, 'Look how *avant-garde* we are: ecumenical ministry to hippies—even hippies!' But once a church grew up out of that, they were horrified! The problem . . . was that this new church, the Free Church, found in those very pages a manifesto for human liberation, a radical Jesus, a Good News for its own problems.'

The eucharistic rite of Berkeley, the Freedom Meal, speaks of 'Jesus our Liberator' and of the cup as 'the unending Constitution of a new society in my blood, poured out for liberation from your guilt.' The Litany of Intercession prays for 'the global movement of peace and liberation, the Church of Jesus incognito'. The Dismissal runs: 'Go in peace and love. Serve God with joy. Keep the faith baby. You are the liberated zone.' In Britain, no real Underground Church has emerged, though *The Catonsville Roadrunner* and 'Church' have been modelled very closely on the Berkeley model, even to the point of imitating the very language used. The weakness of this group, however, is that unlike Berkeley, it did not arise out of any real pastoral situation, and, because it is a second-hand movement with imported slogans and borrowed ideas, it does not really relate to anything, and may simply become yet another precious and introverted sect. Indeed, Berkeley itself could easily become very sectarian in its thought and ethos, separated from the rest of the church as from the mass of the common people.

A third direction which the post-drug spiritual movement has taken is that of fundamentalist Christianity. There has been a growth of groups like the 'Jesus Freaks' which *Nova* described as 'fanatical Christian Hippies'. They include the Children of God commune, founded by Jonathan Levi in Missippi, the God Squad, and Arthur Blessit's centre in Sunset Strip, Los Angeles. In many respects, the Jesus movement is well within the traditions of American revivalism. But its importance lies in two specific aspects. The first is that, unlike many evangelicals like David Wilkerson, the externals and language of the hippy culture are not rejected. The second is that, unlike most forms of evangelical Christianity, the Jesus people are highly critical and intolerant of the mainstream churches and their compromise with Mammon. They represent a radical break with the idea of Christianity as a bulwark of the American way of life. Thus in a sense they can be seen as a revolutionary force. But they are a revival of a tradition notable for its intolerance and its irrationality. In terms of spirituality, surely they are a regression.

One of the convictions which unites all the spiritual movements which we have seen is the belief in a coming age of spirit. Charles Reich in *The Greening of America* looks to a new age of consciousness which 'seeks restoration of the non-material elements of man's existence, the elements like the natural environment and the spiritual.' *Hair* sings of 'the dawning of the Age of Aquarius'. Leary and Cohen, while they disagree about the value of psychedelic drugs, agree that profound changes in consciousness are leading to a spiritual revolution. Radical drop-outs, influenced by Marcuse, speak of liberation in terms both of the individual and of the political structure. The astrologers tell of the planetary influences. Christians in many denominations are witnessing the revival of pentecostalism, and seeking the 'baptism of the Holy Spirit'.

I believe that we are seeing a revival of gnosticism, and of magic and superstition. It would be quite false to see all the signs of spiritual change to be healthy signs. There is a good deal of very unbalanced and deranged mysticism about in the Underground: gnostic ideas of a purely psychic illuminism; morbid interest in the occult and extrasensory powers; involvement with witchcraft and satanism. Even the apparently innocuous interest in flying saucers and astrology can hardly be seen as rational, and some of what goes by the name of mysticism can properly be described as magic and superstition. This is an age in which 'many false spirits have gone out into the world', an age of deep spiritual confusion. But it is an age in which many people are searching for the reality of true prayer and contemplation. The writings of a contemplative monk like Thomas Merton have obviously touched the needs of many in our generation, just as the works of Teilhard de Chardin have brought many to an awareness of spirituality. The harvest is certainly plenteous.

The labourers, however, are few, because we have largely missed the significance of these spiritual occurrences. Spiritual things are spiritually discerned, and contemporary Christianity is profoundly lacking in spiritual perception. We have been so absorbed with changing our image and becoming 'relevant', 'involved' and active, that we have lost our grip on our primary concern, the attainment of the Vision of God. Yet it is God whom men are seeking, and it is only a Church renewed and directed by the Holy Spirit which will be capable of guiding the present spiritual ferment and leading it to fulfilment.

One of my predecessors at St Anne's Soho was Father Gilbert Shaw. He was a great spiritual director and contemplative, and after leaving Soho he became Warden of the Sisters of the Love of God who have been a tremendous support to us throughout our work. Though he died in 1967, the year in which I went to Soho, his awareness of the needs of the present was very great. In one of his papers on prayer, he wrote:

It is vital that we should understand the changes of our age, and we can only do so if our prayer goes deep enough to root us in the unchangeability of God. If our eyes are fixed on him, then however violent the changes, we are not limited by ideas conditioned by the past or the present. We can help the present age by asking the right questions to enable people to see their need, and by standing firm in the stability of prayer to bring in God's true purpose . . . In this confidence we can face the night that has come upon the Church, knowing it has a purpose of purification, a purification necessary for bringing us back to root principles.